EMPLOYEE EXPERIENCE DESIGN

DEAN E. CARTER   SAMANTHA GADD   MARK LEVY

EMPLOYEE EXPERIENCE DESIGN

HOW TO CO-CREATE WORK WHERE PEOPLE *AND* ORGANIZATIONS THRIVE

WILEY

Copyright © 2026 by John Wiley & Sons, Inc. All rights reserved, including rights for text and data mining and training of artificial intelligence technologies or similar technologies.

Published by John Wiley & Sons, Inc., Hoboken, New Jersey.

No part of this publication may be reproduced, stored in a retrieval system, or transmitted in any form or by any means, electronic, mechanical, photocopying, recording, scanning, or otherwise, except as permitted under Section 107 or 108 of the 1976 United States Copyright Act, without either the prior written permission of the Publisher, or authorization through payment of the appropriate per-copy fee to the Copyright Clearance Center, Inc., 222 Rosewood Drive, Danvers, MA 01923, (978) 750-8400, fax (978) 750-4470, or on the web at www.copyright.com. Requests to the Publisher for permission should be addressed to the Permissions Department, John Wiley & Sons, Inc., 111 River Street, Hoboken, NJ 07030, (201) 748-6011, fax (201) 748-6008, or online at http://www.wiley.com/go/permission.

The manufacturer's authorized representative according to the EU General Product Safety Regulation is Wiley-VCH GmbH, Boschstr. 12, 69469 Weinheim, Germany, e-mail: Product_Safety@wiley.com.

Trademarks: Wiley and the Wiley logo are trademarks or registered trademarks of John Wiley & Sons, Inc. and/or its affiliates in the United States and other countries and may not be used without written permission. All other trademarks are the property of their respective owners. John Wiley & Sons, Inc. is not associated with any product or vendor mentioned in this book.

Limit of Liability/Disclaimer of Warranty: While the publisher and the authors have used their best efforts in preparing this work, including a review of the content of the work, neither the publisher nor the authors make any representations or warranties with respect to the accuracy or completeness of the contents of this work and specifically disclaim all warranties, including without limitation any implied warranties of merchantability or fitness for a particular purpose. No warranty may be created or extended by sales representatives, written sales materials, or promotional statements for this work. The fact that an organization, website, or product is referred to in this work as a citation and/or potential source of further information does not mean that the publisher and authors endorse the information or services the organization, website, or product may provide or recommendations it may make. This work is sold with the understanding that the publisher is not engaged in rendering professional services. The advice and strategies contained herein may not be suitable for your situation. You should consult with a specialist where appropriate. Further, readers should be aware that websites listed in this work may have changed or disappeared between when this work was written and when it is read. Neither the publisher nor authors shall be liable for any loss of profit or any other commercial damages, including but not limited to special, incidental, consequential, or other damages.

For general information on our other products and services or for technical support, please contact our Customer Care Department within the United States at (800) 762-2974, outside the United States at (317) 572-3993 or fax (317) 572-4002.

Wiley also publishes its books in a variety of electronic formats. Some content that appears in print may not be available in electronic formats. For more information about Wiley products, visit our website at www.wiley.com.

Library of Congress Cataloging-in-Publication Data is Available:

ISBN: 9781394329588 (Cloth)
ISBN: 9781394329595 (ePub)
ISBN: 9781394329601 (ePDF)

Cover Design: Emma Sygrove-Savill
Author Photos: Courtesy of the Authors

SKY10132846_120225

To every employee who has never been asked—your voice matters.
To the leaders brave enough to listen—thank you for making work better for everyone.

Contents

PART I   **Imagine**   1

Chapter 1   The $100 Bill   3
Seeing Value Others Overlook

Chapter 2   Hardball Objections, Straight Answers   9

Chapter 3   The North Star   21
The EXD Guiding Principle

Chapter 4   A Conversation with Beth Grous   35
The Impact of Trust and Humanity, and the Courage of Everyday Leaders

PART II   **Prepare**   47

Chapter 5   Mindsets   49
Seven Mindsets for Employee Experience Design

Chapter 6   A Conversation with Kirsty Lloyd   63
How Empathy and Feedback Became Cultural Anchors at Scale

PART III   **Design**   77

Chapter 7   Culture Check   79
Moments That Matter and Moments of Truth

Chapter 8	Three Frameworks	87
	A Structure for Achieving Meaningful Design	
Chapter 9	The Double Diamond	109
	A Proven Design Method	

PART IV Experiment — 137

Chapter 10	The EX Blueprint	139
	Letting Everyone See the Big Picture	
Chapter 11	A Conversation with Melanie Rosenwasser	145
	Bringing UX Rigor to EX: It's a Product, Not a Perk	

PART V Measure — 159

Chapter 12	Metrics That Matter	161
	Taking the Pulse of Your Organization	
Chapter 13	A Conversation with Greg Pryor	175
	Turning Experience into Intelligence and Then into Impact	

PART VI Celebrate/Extend — 187

Chapter 14	A Conversation with Michelle Bonfilio	189
	The Emotional Core of Employee Experience Design	
Chapter 15	Making EXD Your Own	205
	Final Wisdom and What Grows over Time	

Postscript: A Personal Reflection from the Authors — *211*
Acknowledgments — *213*
About the Authors — *219*
Index — *223*

PART I Imagine

1

The $100 Bill

Seeing Value Others Overlook

Books like this one can feel a bit impersonal, but even though we are not sitting across from you, we're pretty sure that we know a little bit about you:

- You're a **leader of people** or take initiative to lead in your organization;
- You are tired of the traditional approach HR has taken in driving their initiatives into the organization;
- You are open-minded and **looking for ways to improve your organization**, or else you would not be reading this book;
- You've probably been around the block a few times and have **seen plenty of fads come and go**; and
- You have a **highly developed BS meter**.

How did we do? If this sounds like you, we're going to have a great time together.

You'll hear much more about us in the following pages, but it's important for you to know this: The three of us collectively have more than 75 years of experience in HR/EX and other leadership roles in organizations of all sizes—and we have super-sensitive BS meters, too.

Our purpose in writing this book is to give you insights that you can immediately use to improve your organization.

Because you've been around the block, right away we have a challenge on our hands: You've probably heard of "Employee Experience" or "EX." We'll be taking you through an approach to EX that is next level, and known as **Employee Experience Design**, or EXD. Relatively few organizations have fully implemented EXD, and the benefits are huge for those that have.

Our further goal is to talk with you, practitioner to practitioner, leader to leader. We don't need to tell you how hard it is to implement an initiative in your organization—no doubt you have the scars to show for it.

That means we've set the bar high for this book: We need to tell you at least a few things even you didn't know and that you can use right away in your own unique circumstances. It's a tall order, but we're up to the challenge.

It's Not Just a Book—It's a Handbook

Books are great, but often a handbook is even better, and that's what we've created here. Because we don't know your particular situation, we've laid out this handbook in a way that you can jump around to suit your interests, and easily refer back to sections as you work through challenges in your organization.

In this handbook, we try to cover three important aspects of EXD:

1. **The Why.** Skeptical people are the best: They have lots of questions and need convincing before they'll get onboard with anything. This first part of the handbook covers why EXD is so important and addresses many legitimate—and tough—questions you may have. We also talk about how EXD leads to better business outcomes.
2. **The What.** We have supported EXD in hundreds of organizations worldwide. This part of the handbook gives you the important mindset shifts, principles, decisions, actions, and tools you can use to implement EXD in your organization.
3. **The How.** The greatest insights are useless if they never get implemented. But organizations are like fingerprints: no two are exactly alike, even though there are similarities. In this part, we give you what you need to know in order to make EXD work for your particular circumstances and for your role in the organization.

You're in for a Treat

We know literally thousands of professionals in HR/EX and other leadership roles, and some of those people shine like bright stars. They're special in at least two ways: they've implemented EXD in difficult circumstances, and they're great at telling their story.

Not only do we have full conversations with several stars in this handbook, but you'll hear from many others in the context of certain points we make throughout these pages.

The $100 Bill

We'll get into lots of hard-hitting questions soon, but right away we want to address what you might be thinking now:

> If EXD is so great, why hasn't it gone viral? Why doesn't every organization use it?

Fair question, and it's where our parable comes in. Imagine that a wealthy person lost a $100 bill in a snowstorm. It landed in a gutter and got plowed into a pile of snow. Some days later, just a portion of that bill became visible in the snow and mud.

- The vast majority of people walk right by because they're busy, late for a meeting, on the phone, whatever.
- A few people see something muddy and green, but hey it's a thing in the gutter.
- Perhaps hundreds of people will walk by before someone stops, takes the time to recognize it, and makes the further effort to fish it out of the mud. The value of the bill was always there, but only a fraction of people will be in a position to both recognize it and take action.

EXD is the $100 bill. The mud is all the years of annual surveys and shiny new tech tools that obscure the true value of EXD, not to mention the barrage of information that buries us in more mud each week. If we can see past all that, EXD is there for the taking.

You're the one who paused and picked up what you saw as valuable, in the form of this handbook. What you'll learn can be transformative for your organization and for your career, as you'll soon see. It could even be worth millions.

Who Are We?

We are Dean E. Carter, Samantha Gadd, and Mark Levy. How three people from different continents and companies ended up writing a book together is a story we'll share later. And instead of writing out lengthy bios, which change regularly, we thought it would be more interesting to describe some of our collective professional experiences in no particular order:

- Sold adult diapers for Procter & Gamble.
- Worked as a labor-law attorney for a company where our job was to catch people making mistakes.
- Was CHRO for a 240,000-person company.
- Worked as a travel agent.
- Was an area trainer.
- Currently and in the past, have been on the boards of many companies.
- Lived and worked in Paris (very different organizational approach in France).
- Created a leadership development program.
- Dean of an academy for future heads of HR.
- Global head of talent at a branding and design firm.
- Learned how to sell and adjust eyewear.
- Built a woman-owned consultancy that's the largest of its kind in New Zealand.
- CHRO for iconic worldwide brands like Patagonia, Levi's, Gap, Eddie Bauer, Best Buy, Airbnb, Technicolor, Fossil.
- Have had the following departments reporting to one or more of us:
  - HR
  - Food and facilities
  - Safety and security
  - Wellness
  - Social impact

- Finance
- Real estate
- Legal
- Family services

Although the three of us come from very different backgrounds, we share a common belief—HR and other roles that affect the experiences of employees are absolutely critical to the success of every organization. We also know that most of these roles have a pile of work, competing priorities, and limited resources.

This handbook can be an antidote to that situation when you apply what you learn here. We'll guide you through a path to do more that does not involve the typical "solution" of adding more to your plate or asking for a larger budget.

What EXD and This Handbook Are Not

Let's look at what else EXD and this guide are not:

> **This is not a disguised pitch for expensive consulting services.** On the one hand, it's true that we haven't found a way to condense three careers' worth of knowledge and experience into one volume. But we can guarantee you this: After finishing this guide, you'll have clarity on the specific path you can take to implement what you learn here, with nothing further to buy.
>
> Because we want to support you in ways that extend beyond this handbook, we will occasionally point you to a URL where you can leave your email address and we will send you (at no charge) additional reading or resources like handouts.
>
> **EXD is not a silver bullet.** You won't hear us making any claims along the lines of: "Five simple steps to revolutionize your business!" EXD takes real work to pull off—sometimes hard work by you and others. There will also be setbacks because we both know that real progress never happens in a straight line. But as you'll see, you're very likely to wish you had known of this approach much earlier in your career.

EXD is not "one size fits all." That's both bad and good news. The bad is the work necessary to adapt EXD to your organization. It will take some practice to get full benefits from it. As you'll read later, we've certainly made our share of mistakes along the way. The good news is you will soon have something that's tailored to your unique situation and that delivers a substantial ROI on your efforts.

Finally, this is not a "once and done" deal where you can form a team, get a new logo designed, and then check it off your list. We think you'll agree that we live in a continuous state of change. Whether it's the government, economy, pandemics, competitors—you name it— the only reliable touchstone is change. EXD is not a quick or new shiny tool but a mindset, as we'll talk much more about. You'll find yourself applying that mindset again and again to meet whatever is the next challenge.

We decided to write this book because practically every week, one or another of us is traveling somewhere in the world, advising organizations, giving keynotes, or implementing EXD. We get asked certain questions over and over, and there never seems to be enough time to do justice to the answers. Albert Einstein once said that the goal is to reach "simplicity on the other side of complexity." In other words, if you really understand something, you should be able to boil it down to the essential principles. This book is our attempt to do just that.

2

Hardball Objections, Straight Answers

"It ain't what you don't know that gets you into trouble. It's what you know for sure that just ain't so."

—*Attributed to Mark Twain*

As we said in the last chapter, we like skeptics. They're the folks that don't quickly salute the next initiative because they have questions, and sometimes lots of them. They may take a while to be convinced of something because they want a solid foundation of understanding.

Of course, you can tell we're big fans of Employee Experience Design, or we wouldn't have written this book. But in this chapter, we want to focus on people who may have a number of concerns or objections.

First, Some Definitions

We'll get into the tough questions in a moment, but it makes sense first for us to get some basic definitions out of the way. First, when we refer to "employees," we're being inclusive to mean full-time employees, part-time ones, contractors, volunteers—people who work together to deliver on a business promise.

Next, "Employee Experience" or "EX" is not an initiative or set of tools—it's a combination of three things:

1. **It's a mindset.** We'll discuss this in detail in Chapter 5;
2. **It's ways of working.** Multiple chapters will give you the methods we've used; and
3. **It's organizing what was the HR function** beyond the traditional responsibility or scope.

It also is the combined thoughts, feelings, and interactions that employees have at work. EX can be great, terrible, or somewhere in between, and every organization has EX, whether it recognizes it or not.

In this handbook, we focus on "Employee Experience Design" or "EXD." Extremely few organizations have fully developed EXD efforts, even though they may think they have them. (To complicate things a bit, early on, the term "EX" referred to both the design and the outcome. The two terms later evolved to mean different things.)

The great power of the word "design" is that it refers to intentionality. EXD is the proactive and intentional process of creating and improving employee experiences. As Steve Jobs said: "Design is not just what it looks like and feels like. Design is how it works." Here's the very most succinct way we can state it:

> Employee Experience Design is designing *with* people and not *for* them.

If you read this handbook and remember nothing else beyond those 11 words—and you implement them—you will be ahead of the vast majority of organizations on the planet. That's the essence of the book. There you have it.

For too long, leaders in HR and elsewhere have made decisions independently from what employees think or need. They've done so without leveraging their valuable input to determine the priorities that will help them to deliver on organization goals and the customer experience. As a result, they've pushed their agenda into the organization, rather than leveraging the voice and input of employees. They did things TO their employees, instead of WITH them. This is the monumental change that EXD is all about.

We mentioned Einstein in the last chapter. He came up with the most famous equation ever, which is $E = mc^2$. We are not claiming to be Einsteins, but here's the similarity: It's easy to write out a definition of something, but the real effort is in understanding how and when to apply it. The rest of this handbook is devoted to benefitting from our experience in how to design with people and not for them.

Now for Those Hardball Objections

You and we all know how the game works in organizations: Some new project comes down to us from on high. We may be given the opportunity to ask questions, but the expectation is that we're on board and only asking for clarification. Those soft questions can be fine, but what we want to do now is ask some tough ones, then answer them.

"EXD is nothing but a fad. Even worse, it's a fad that already has run its course. I heard about it even before COVID."

There is some truth to this objection, but only a little. One of us (Mark) coined the term "EX" while at Airbnb in 2013. (Much more on my time at Airbnb later.) Therefore, EX (later EXD) has indeed been around since before COVID.

You might be interested in how the concept of EX started. I was interviewing at Airbnb and Brian Chesky, one of the founders, shared that everything he'd heard about HR he didn't particularly like. Brian asked if we could do things differently. He had just written an article in *Medium*, called: "Don't Fuck Up the Culture,"[1] and essentially told me that's the main purpose of the role he was looking to fill. This was music to my ears. I shared that he had a CX team that focused on feedback from customers to create a better travel experience. Why not have an EX team that focused on the feedback of our employees to create a better employee experience? If we treat our employees the way we want them to treat our customers (in our case, it's the host that delivers belonging to our guests), then we will create a virtuous cycle.

---

[1] https://medium.com/@bchesky/dont-fuck-up-the-culture-597cde9ee9d4

Back to fads: Whether something is a fad or not has to do with who adopts it and whether it's deeply integrated or merely toyed with. Years ago, we heard that the "quality movement" was going to be a "requirement of doing business" in the near future. Some businesses like Toyota fully adopted the principles while other manufacturers got on the bandwagon with signage and a little training, only to drop off soon after.

We've seen this phenomenon more recently with remote work. Some companies had strong remote capabilities before 2020, and then COVID hit. Everyone had to go remote, like it or not, which became a huge challenge for HR. Later came the backlash, with some organizations unplugging remote work and requiring 100 percent return to office. Some organizations have continued to be fully remote and others have found their sweet spot with a hybrid mix of remote and in person.

So, were the quality movement and remote work just fads? You can only answer that at the individual organization level. Even though it's a saying, it's also true: You get out of something what you put in. If an organization adopts the latest fad simply because it's what everyone else is doing—without alignment to strategy or business impact—then those efforts are fads for them. In contrast, another organization may adopt far fewer initiatives but does a great job of deeply learning, applying, and adapting them to its needs and connecting them to key business outcomes. It's that latter type of organization that will go the furthest with EXD.

> "No offense, but this is window dressing BS. The real work of HR is recruiting, training, compensation, and policy work. Those are the things that MUST get done in the organization, and we only have enough bandwidth to do the must-haves."

There is no question that recruiting and the other functions are key to HR's work. Here's the thing: EXD is not something you *add to your plate*; it's a mindset you use to look at what's on your plate in the first place. It's how you work with your employees, leveraging them to help set priorities and design solutions.

Let's take policy development as an example, and the reactive DEI initiative that happened after the George Floyd murder. HR departments and C-suites across the country were immediately tasked with developing DEI policies. What often happened was that Black employees were not involved from the outset of the project and not asked for their thoughts about how best to approach it. Instead, policies were created and announced, pronto.

Sure, there may have been messaging to the effect of: "We'd love to hear your feedback," but the subtext is usually pretty clear: *We're the leaders and this is our policy. Do you have a problem with that?* Only the boldest few tend to speak up with comments.

It does not involve extra work to apply the EXD approach to a project. On the contrary: Designing a policy with employees and not for them means that you might have more ideas from the outset. You'll then go through fewer drafts to reach a workable policy. EXD can result in less on your plate, not more.

EXD can result in less on your plate, not more.

> "The fact is, we don't need EXD. We always have way more applicants than we have positions to fill. If a person can't get on board with our approach, it's easy to get someone who will."

EXD is an advantage and not a necessity the way paying the electricity bill is. As we already said, plenty of organizations will do "business as usual" without ever designing things with employees.

But let's look more closely at the situation of having more applicants than open positions. For most positions, there is a type of bell curve regarding who applies. At one end of the curve are the clearly non-qualified applicants. Then there's the big center section (a.k.a. the "pig in the python") where applicants are mostly qualified. At the top of the curve are the most-desirable applicants. They're extremely well qualified and they (and employers) know it. Often these top applicants have more than one job offer and can take their pick.

Now consider job offers from two organizations for this same candidate. One organization makes a big deal of its EXD approach and the other doesn't mention it because it doesn't follow EXD. Might this be a factor that influences the candidate? EXD can become an edge in hiring, and can take even more off the plate of HR because it becomes easier to fill positions. In later chapters, you'll hear some great stories about this competitive edge.

> "EXD is a luxury we can't afford. We're in a cutthroat industry where many of our competitors are overseas, and they have zero interest in focusing so much on their employees. And customers seem to buy their stuff all the time!"

We have personal experience with highly competitive industries like apparel, electronics, and mail-order retail. It's true that foreign competitors can often sell products for less than domestic companies can even make them.

In cases like that, EXD can become not a burden but an advantage. Let's consider a call center, for example. It's common for sales managers to create scripts for phone reps to use when selling products and services. Those managers may have substantial sales experience, or it could be that they inherited the department in a shake-up.

What's not common is for sales managers to spend the time to determine if some phone reps have come up with even more effective approaches to answering objections than what was in the original script. Perhaps a recent hire had experience elsewhere and brought that knowledge to the call center.

If the manager makes a conscious effort to harvest these best approaches and then spreads them to the other reps, the center's call time and closing rate could improve at no additional cost. It might even result in higher retention in the call center, given that reps' successful approaches are being recognized and there's more of a team atmosphere.

> "EXD may work for over-funded startups that want to coddle their employees. We have real work to do and a real budget to meet."

We've all heard the stories about companies hiring chefs from Michelin-starred restaurants to serve gourmet meals, "pawternity leave" for adopting pets, nap pods, and so on. If these benefits were cooked up in the C-suite because someone thought a certain benefit would be cool, then that's a problem. If instead a benefit was designed with employees, it might be a smart move. You'll hear more later about how we handled a difficult issue at Patagonia with no hit to the budget.

EXD is not about upping the ante and outdoing your competitors with lavish benefits. It's about working with employees to add, leave alone, or sometimes drop benefits—among many other aspects of work—based upon a methodical, joint evaluation. Later, we go into a lot of detail about what that collaboration looks like.

> "It would be nice to experiment with some of this stuff, but I have way bigger fish to fry. We're already understaffed. There's no way I can find the time to do it."

Embedded in that statement is the classic situation that leaders typically assume: If something needs to get done, they're the ones who will need to do it. That's sometimes the case, like when the CHRO must deliver a presentation to the board. But EXD involves designing with employees, who can take some of the responsibility off your shoulders.

One of the great things about EXD is it means you no longer need to have all the answers yourself. And when you implement EXD across multiple projects, the time savings for you can become significant. Of course, EXD is not about delegating projects to others; you'll still be involved.

EXD is it means you no longer need to have all the answers yourself.

There's a related objection that we sometimes hear, and it's that "It's not the right time" to implement anything now. It may be true that some times during the year are blackout periods when it's "all hands on deck." But consider how easy it is to say that it's not a good time: When business and the economy are booming, it's easy to say: "We need to wait until things slow down." Then when things slow down, it's easy to say: "Bad time right now; we need to focus on making our numbers, so we have to wait until things pick up."

> "EXD sounds interesting, but you don't know the people I report to. All they care about is getting stuff out the door and meeting their numbers. They set the agenda, not me."

There is no question that the fastest way to implement EXD is if you have support from the top. It's also true that your organization's leadership may have seen too many initiatives come and go—and may even have contributed to the perception that they're just fads.

In our experience, the next-best thing to having the C-suite on board from the outset is to start *somewhere* in the organization. Let's say that you're the first one in your organization to be reading this handbook and you end up liking what you learned. In later chapters, we'll talk about how you can begin to use and benefit from EXD, no matter where you are in the organization. As you'll see, it doesn't need to start with an initiative that you must get buy-in for.

> **"Sorry, but EXD is just a bad idea. We'll lose control and besides, we'll never be able to deliver on employees' wish lists. You don't know our employees!"**

Multiple items to unpack here. Because we're being straight with you, we'll tell you about one downside to EXD in some organizations. Sometimes people want their plate to be overflowing, because they equate it with being in control.

They may have spent years working their way up the ladder and now are in a senior position. It's always been a top-down organization where policy is made in the corner office and issued to the troops. Now EXD comes along, and they think: *I earned this position! Now I'm supposed to dilute my power and design things with people sometimes many levels below me? It's not gonna happen.*

With this sort of person, the trick is to let them see over time that they gain much more in terms of meeting organizational objectives than they give up. What might initially seem like dilution of their control doesn't occur: They still have the position, and their team is working better than ever to meet their KPIs. Less can be more.

The other fear mentioned above is what you hear some parents say about little kids: "If you give them an inch, they'll take a mile!" We've been involved in EXD in hundreds of organizations and can tell you that this fear doesn't materialize if you use some common sense.

You don't announce that the organization now has unlimited funds and ask for wish lists. Instead, you start with the context of the project: Maybe it's that we need to design a new policy for remote vs. in-person work; or we're beginning the design of new space that we'll be moving into in the fall. It could also be a problem to solve like how food costs have gone through the roof and we want to come together to figure out a solution that works best for everyone.

> *We've found that with rare exceptions, when adults are treated like adults, they become helpful partners at work.*

▎ "We already focus on employee experience."

Maybe you do; we don't know your organization. Here's what we've found: Most organizations do little to no Employee Experience Design. They may have a suggestion box or do an annual survey, but that is not EXD.

A suggestion box is better than nothing if in fact someone reads the suggestions and acts on them. Unfortunately, suggestion boxes can sometimes be mistaken for trash cans in terms of how they're dealt with. Even if suggestions are genuinely solicited and valued, it's a passive system that does not take the place of actively seeking employee involvement across the full spectrum of employee experience.

As for annual surveys, they're next to useless. They are like having someone take a photo for you of downtown Chicago in July in advance of your trip there. Then you spend the rest of the year planning your trip and packing your shorts and swimsuit—for when you arrive in Chicago in February, when the temp is below zero.

Annual employee surveys are a snapshot of a moment in time, but an organization is instead a dynamic environment that's continuously changing on a dozen different dimensions. Just think of all the things that happen in a year: changes in leadership; reorganizations of departments; external forces like elections, regulations,

> *Annual employee surveys are a snapshot of a moment in time, but an organization is instead a dynamic environment that's continuously changing on a dozen different dimensions.*

and the economy affecting your ability to meet your objectives; and so on. And we're going to comprehensively and accurately measure all of that with a single snapshot in time?

You need to create systems that are just as frequent and dynamic as the environment you're attempting to evaluate. In a sense, the survey is worse than doing nothing because it can become window dressing for saying: "We listen to our employees." At least if you don't do one, you can't hide behind it.

Let's just say for a moment that an organization does do a legitimate form of EXD on occasion. The typical problem is those operative words: "On occasion." For example, it may be that HR has done a good job of drilling down and focusing on life cycle moments, like encouraging qualified candidates to apply. They might have co-created an effective referral system for employees to tell their friends about job postings. Maybe it goes even further: They've enlisted the help of employees to help with the interview process, to make sure the candidate would work well with the people and culture of this organization. (You will hear later about the great system we built at Airbnb along these lines.)

Anyway, these are solid examples of using EXD during the hiring process, and it may even include later elements like onboarding. The problem is that these employment moments may span a few initial weeks of the several years that an employee might be with an organization—maybe one or two percent of the overall job experience. It's a good place to start, but it's not enough.

Of course, it's unrealistic to expect that anyone can transform all aspects of an organization overnight, so you do need to start somewhere. But when you have the EXD mindset, with each next project and each update of existing policies, it's another opportunity to design with employees.

Is this going overboard? Consider Apple. Steve Wozniak and Steve Jobs started with redesigning the personal computer. Before long, the same design mindset was applied to the iPod, then iPhone, iPad, the mouse, monitors, watches, and so on. Design is a way of thinking at Apple, at Patagonia (about which you'll hear more later), and at other legendary brands.

It's not that the brands are first legendary and then adopt great design; it's the other way around—they become legendary by beginning with design. In whatever is your own corner of the world, you can do the same thing by applying design thinking to employee experience.

> *It's not that the brands are first legendary and then adopt great design; it's the other way around—they become legendary by beginning with design.*

We hope we've shown you that EXD is powerful and can even be transformative, but it's not "too good to be true." We'll be giving you lots of tested and proven approaches to challenges, but none will involve "weird tricks they don't want you to know," as so many social media ads promise. Instead, it's an approach that takes some work to learn and then to apply. Even so, it's not rocket science; it's about listening, collaboration, and a two-way dialogue. You're already along that journey by reading this handbook.

Let's next talk about a topic that's so important, all your efforts with EXD will be worthless without it.

Chapter Summary

Employee Experience (EX) is a combination of mindset, ways of working, and organizing the HR function, encompassing all thoughts, feelings, and interactions employees have at work.

Employee Experience Design (EXD) is the proactive and intentional process of creating and improving employee experiences. It's all about designing *with* people and not *for* them.

It's true that any initiative can be a fad if the organization doesn't take it seriously and stick with it. When EXD is aligned with organizational outcomes, it can become a vital component of growth. (Much more on this in the next chapter.)

EXD is not window dressing, and it doesn't always mean extra work; it's a mindset that can make existing tasks like policy development more efficient and effective from the outset.

EXD offers a competitive edge in hiring, particularly for top talent, because it influences candidates' choices beyond compensation.

EXD is not a luxury or only for over-funded startups. It can be a cost-effective advantage by harvesting best practices and optimizing existing resources.

3

The North Star

The EXD Guiding Principle

Organizations come in infinite shapes and sizes, but there is at least one common denominator: They were created to accomplish some goal. At the mega-end of the spectrum, maybe a Fortune 50 company spun off a unit that will be funded with a few billion and whose goal is to build an AI agent to aid in pharmaceutical research.

At the small, other end of the spectrum, maybe someone created a Kickstarter campaign to make adjustable-focus eyeglasses so people without the means don't have to buy expensive prescription ones. That effort has turned into a nonprofit that employs 100 people. Both of these organizations have a clear reason for being, and that reason can further be broken down into organizational outcomes.

One reason why some initiatives become mere fleeting fads is they are not tied to the key outcomes needed to further the goal of the organization. We refer to the "North Star" in the chapter title because it relates to the next principle of Employee Experience Design:

▎ For EXD to be effective, it must be tied to organizational outcomes.

Those outcomes comprise the North Star. That link between an EXD project and the outcomes provides a solid foundation that's explainable at any level of the organization.

Let's look at six areas where EXD efforts can support organizational outcomes.

1. **Attracting the people we need.** As we mentioned earlier, the top talent in any industry usually has their pick of multiple job offers. Competitive industries may be able to sweeten the compensation offers to such people, but only up to a point, after which other factors come into play. These people will query their network of friends and alumni to find out what it's really like to work somewhere. They'll also see what social media and outfits like Glassdoor have to say about the employer.

   When I (Mark) was at Airbnb and our team had invested a lot of effort in EXD, one day Glassdoor informed us that our employees had rated Airbnb to be #1 on its list of "The Best Places to Work" in the entire United States in 2016. I'm particularly proud of our great team because the award is not something you can spend money and create a task force to apply for; it's earned through anonymous reviews of our employee experience. By the way, at the time, about half of Airbnb's new hires came from referrals.

   Even if an organization does not win a Glassdoor award, it can benefit from glowing reviews on Glassdoor from employees and positive statements on LinkedIn and Reddit, among other similar platforms.

   Sometimes fixing the employee experience is worth more than money. We know of a case where a highly qualified person interviewed at one of the most-famous venture capital firms in the world. This company didn't just generate returns—it minted fortunes. The CHRO lamented that they lost this prized candidate because their interview process was simply too slow and cumbersome. The candidate grew tired of waiting and accepted a job at a competitor. Applying EXD to improving this process would be a no-brainer.

2. **Retaining employees.** Here are two stories from my (Dean) time at Patagonia as CHRO (I was there for more than eight years):

As you no doubt know, Patagonia is famous for its useful and rugged clothing. We didn't hire fashion designers to make our clothes; instead, we hired "dirtbags" (in the words of Yvon Chouinard, the founder) who were passionate at a variety of activities like rock climbing, surfing, skiing, and so on. They helped to design the kind of clothing they personally wanted to use and that worked best.

Our headquarters was in Ventura, California, close to the beach. Literally, it was common for some employees to drop what they were doing and catch some waves if word got around that the surf was up. (This was not frowned upon but encouraged.) However, we started to notice that the employee experience of skiers and mountain climbers was taking a hit. They were just as passionate as the surfers and just as vital to our clothing lines, but Ventura is not known for its snow-packed mountains.

To be more specific, some of them would quit, and others explained to me they just couldn't stuff in much mountain time when the drive was so long. Sure, they could use vacation days to create long weekends, but that burned up their vacation for the rest of the year.

They said it would make all the difference if they just had one more day on some weekends. Our goal became to figure out a way to create some three-day weekends without harming productivity or costing the company too much.

In talking about it with employees, we decided to try the following system: Instead of the employees working eight-hour days, they'd work nine-hour days. Over a two-week period, every second Friday they would have off work. In addition, for the other Friday, they could work half a day from home and have the other half off. We tried it, recognizing that we might have to make adjustments if it didn't work adequately for the business or for employees.

Our turnover problem disappeared. Not only did it disappear, but get this: We worked with a local university to help us do surveys.

We asked some of the standard questions relating to engagement and productivity, but we also asked a few unusual questions:

1. "As a result of this benefit, do you have a better relationship with your spouse?" 90 percent said they did.
2. "As a result of this benefit, do you have more time to spend with your children?" 72 percent said they did.
3. 90 percent said they had more time to go to the doctor and dentist. (After all, most doctors and dentists don't work weekends.)

What did this change cost the company? Zero. And besides retention going through the roof, productivity went up slightly. When I speak these days to audiences around the globe, I'll often ask for a show of hands to the question: "How many of you have a better relationship with your spouse as a result of work?" Almost never does a hand go up. But we made it happen at Patagonia and it didn't cost us a dime. In fact, if you consider the hidden costs of turnover, our joint solution saved the company money.

Remember that in Chapter 1, we said that EXD is not a once-and-done proposition. That was true with this change for clothing designers, because when we implemented this policy for them, other folks like in the retail stores and warehouse saw the benefits of this innovation and naturally wanted in. That's fair, but we couldn't just clone the solution for them, because we couldn't shut down retail stores or the warehouse every other Friday; so, we came up with adjustments that worked for them.

This is the sort of project that when you see how people come together to design a solution that meets everyone's needs—you get hooked. You never want to go back to the old ways of rationalizing that "turnover is a fact of life—we'll just get some new designers." You'll begin to look for where else in the organization you can pull off a similar win-win.

Here's the second Patagonia story about retention. We had several women in senior roles in the company. To be more specific, some of them were in roles that required travel, and some of those women were nursing mothers.

One woman said: "It was the worst day of my life."

Someone told me what all these women already knew: At the time, airports had no special accommodations for nursing mothers, so the most privacy they could find in order to pump breast milk was to do it in the toilet stall. Then—because of TSA regulations prohibiting the carrying of liquids—they needed to flush their milk down the toilet. One woman said: "It was the worst day of my life."

The alternative for these women was to stay home and not travel for work. That meant someone else took their place, which ultimately had an effect on their career progression relative to others who could travel.

Patagonia was already a pretty forward-thinking organization; for example, it was not uncommon for a woman to be in a board meeting, nursing her baby. Shannon Ellis, an employee in HR, after pouring out her breast milk in the airport during an overseas work trip, thought no woman should have to make that choice again. So, she created what became the "Traveling Companion Benefit." This allowed the nursing mother to travel with her baby and a paid companion, whose role was to assist with caring for the baby while the mother attended to her work responsibilities.

This arrangement eliminated the toilet-stall trauma because the mother could nurse her baby before and after going through TSA and not miss a beat. She didn't need to leave her baby home and store up her milk; now she had the opportunity to learn and grow like everyone else.

This arrangement had a profound effect on nursing women and even on women in general at Patagonia: More nursing women felt like they could take on leadership roles without having to choose between their career and their family. The benefit significantly improved the retention of female employees overall, because they felt supported by the company instead of being told: "Business is business."

This benefit did not noticeably affect our travel or insurance costs, but it was a gigantic ROI for us in terms of retention, goodwill, and attracting other women to the company.

When I left Patagonia and became Chief People Officer at Guild, a startup tech company, the Traveling Companion Benefit was the first thing I implemented there.

3. **EXD increases the chances that initiatives will be successful.** Because we live in an environment of continual change—and sometimes even upheaval—organizations must continually adapt. That means they're usually planning, creating, and implementing initiatives across departments.

We think it's a safe bet that you've been involved in initiatives where a massive amount of time and energy was spent to launch them—and some of them ended up being a complete waste of time. Not only did the desired outcome not happen, but the "dead on arrival" project was demoralizing for everyone who worked on it.

I (Samantha) was contacted by a large organization in New Zealand. They were frustrated because they'd spent a lot of money on more than one leadership development initiative and consultant; they were not seeing any return on investment; and had no buy-in from leaders across the organization. It turns out that they had not worked with these leaders to co-design their own program. (Notice how this phenomenon of "designing for" is not limited to lower-level workers, but can happen anywhere in organizations.)

The buy-in of their next effort was substantially improved when the leaders helped to design it by answering some fundamental questions: "How do you want to be described by people in your area?" and "What are the exact phrases and words that you would like them to use when describing you?"

The better approach is to ask: "Before we begin this initiative, how do we enlist the help of the folks it's going to affect?"

Here's one way to gauge if you are on the right or wrong track when you've developed an initiative and are rolling it out: If you or someone else asks: "How do we get buy-in?" you're on the wrong track. You are closing the doors after the horse has left the barn. The better approach is to ask: "Before we begin this initiative, how do we enlist the help of the folks it's going to affect?"

4. **Coming up with new product ideas.** There is no doubt that the conventional approach to product development often works. Organizations may use a combination of research and development, strategic planning, and market research to develop ideas. However, some legendary companies have also enlisted the creativity of people who became curious and were allowed to run with their ideas.

One great example is in the book, *The Power of Habit*, by Charles Duhigg.[1] He recounts how a scientist at Procter & Gamble was working to develop what's known as an "excipient," which is an inactive substance (like gelatin or starch) that's used in pharmaceuticals. He was a chain smoker and one day when he came home, his wife asked if he had quit smoking. She couldn't smell the usual reeking smoke on his clothes. He had an idea: Did the stuff at the lab eliminate odors? Very long story short—it sure did. It became Febreze and has been responsible for more than a billion dollars of sales.[2]

Other similar discoveries were for Post-it Notes™ and Teflon™. Although it's not a direct example of designing a policy "with and not for" employees, it's an indirect one: "How do we attract scientists and create conditions such that they might come up with their own ideas about how we can succeed?" These are examples of the principle that says: "The answers we seek can often be found in the population we serve."

5. **Improving the performance of teams.** You will hear a lot in Chapter 12 about the right and wrong ways to measure employee experience, including some really surprising insights. But here we want to talk about how listening to employees and addressing their pain points can lead to substantial positive outcomes.

It came to my (Dean's) attention when I was at Guild that one group within the company—the recruiting coordinators ("RCs")—were scoring really low on our bi-weekly energy pulse. They were reporting that they were "exhausted" at a rate much higher than the rest of Guild. To get to the bottom of what was driving this, I did one-on-one discussions and also a focus group.

---

[1] Duhigg, Charles. *The Power of Habit: Why We Do What We Do in Life and Business.* New York: Random House Trade Paperbacks, 2023.
[2] https://www.marketingweek.com/pg-adds-febreze-to-1bn-brand-portfolio/

The RCs were responsible for scheduling interviews between candidates and hiring managers. The problem was that when hiring managers had to cancel an interview, they would tell the RC and expect the RC to tell the candidates about the cancellation. They felt like they were constantly apologizing for schedule changes that were outside of their control and creating a terrible experience for candidates. Conversely, it was easy for the hiring managers to cancel—they didn't have to do the dirty work.

The issues didn't stop there. It was common in town hall meetings to recognize recruiters for new hires, but the RCs never got any spotlight. In an ironic twist, it was the RCs who worked hard to have the candidate experience be positive, when there was no thought to the RC experience. Pardon my language, but they said they felt that "shit rolled downhill to us." They also had even more work when hiring managers sent them incomplete forms. That caused a delay in order to get the forms completed, and the RCs caught heat for the delays.

I asked them: "What do you see as your job?" They said: "We make sure candidates have great experiences." I then asked, "What if your title more closely reflected what you see as your work?" They were delighted. It took no rocket science or task forces to do something about all these issues:

- I mandated that if a hiring manager canceled an interview, that person was responsible for first delivering that news and then rescheduling the candidate.
- I made sure that RCs got some of the public credit for new hires.
- If hiring managers delivered incomplete forms, the recruitment process would be halted until they completed the forms.
- Finally, we changed the title from RC to "Candidate Experience Specialist." Not only was it more descriptive, but it generated more respect.

The RC team went from having the lowest numbers in the organization to being one of the most-energized teams in all of Guild. And it cost zero.

6. **Creating a culture that self-corrects.** You may wonder what on earth we're talking about. It's common for organizations to pay lip service to lofty, inspirational statements. It's also common for those statements to be filed away until the next strategic planning session or the

next town hall when they might be displayed. In the meantime, they're given little thought.

We had a very different culture at Airbnb, which had a mission of creating a world where anyone could belong anywhere. I (Mark) joined the company in 2013, by which time there already was a group known as "Ground Control." I consider them to be the "Secret Sauce" of Airbnb. They were a self-organizing group of people from various disciplines: personal assistants, facilities leaders, site leaders, and so on. They were not cheerleaders—they were curators of the culture.

Ground Control had multiple functions:

- They played a role in shaping the physical spaces where employees worked.
- They were responsible for keeping their finger on the pulse and an ear to the ground, so they knew what employees were thinking and feeling, in order to keep them informed and connected.
- They organized events and activities that fostered community and engagement among employees.
- Ground Control also implemented programs to acknowledge and celebrate employee contributions.
- Finally, they ensured that the mission, values, and behaviors were THE way of working and acting. This greatly helped the democratization of our culture.

The next thing you need to know is the hiring process at Airbnb. Two of the three founders had backgrounds in design, so they applied that approach to the company from the outset. They didn't just let the culture happen, but took steps to determine what they wanted that culture to be as the company grew.

The founders were inspired by the traditional kind of animation that Disney created. It was called "cel animation" where each frame of the animation was a separate handmade drawing. Every frame or "cel" then was intentionally adjusted a little bit, so when they were filmed one after the other and turned into a movie, they blended together to create motion. The founders loved that

> One of our original stated values was "every frame matters."

intentionality and thought it was a good metaphor for what we wanted to do: identify every step of the journey we want to design with our hosts, our guests, and our employees. One of our original stated values was "every frame matters."

As a result, the hiring-interview process had two parts. First was the more conventional piece, where the hiring manager and recruiting staff were expected to find and vet the most qualified candidates for the job. Then came the second set of interviews. These were done by two people who had jobs elsewhere in the organization—not from the hiring manager's department. They interviewed the candidate individually and were not told what position the person was being considered for. In fact, many times they were not given the person's resume or any other material.

The job of these interviewers was to listen for signals around whether the person wanted to join for reasons having to do with the mission of the company. The interviewers also gauged whether the candidate would be aligned with our values, based on answers to behavioral questions about how they approached life and work.

If both these people said yes, then the person was hired. If both said no, the person was not hired. With a split decision, then a third person would interview the candidate without being told that they were the tie breaker.

The original core values interviewers were the founders, and as we grew, they identified culture carriers who became core values interviewers. At scale, it became a full-on program with training and a selection process with hundreds of interviewers across the globe.

In this period, Ground Control and the traditional HR functions reported to me as head of Employee Experience (I had several other units reporting to me as well). We were dead serious about this process. In one case, a very high-profile woman was recruited to interview with us for a top position. She was a big shot on Wall Street and sailed through the first set of interviews. One of the founders really wanted her for the position.

In the course of our conversations, she was told that the next day she'd meet a couple of her potential direct reports. "Why should I do that? I have no interest in that. After all, they'll be reporting to me, not the other way around."

We explained that she could learn a lot about what she would be getting into, as well as get a feel for team cohesion, and we'd like to proceed with the meeting. She said: "Tell you what: I want you to call me part way through the hour and we'll pretend that it's important, so I can bail out of that meeting, OK?"

We said that was not OK. As you can guess, she failed the core values interviews, and we didn't hire her. She went on to a top role in one of the iconic Silicon Valley companies.

> *She failed the core values interviews, and we didn't hire her. She went on to a top role in one of the iconic Silicon Valley companies.*

Was our system flawless? No. Occasionally someone would get through the interview process who turned out not to have joined for the right reason or not to have lived the values. What's surprising is how well it did work, given that we're talking about subjective measures and judgments and not a test about coding ability.

You may wonder: How exactly did we assess for our core values? It was about understanding how the candidate's approach aligned with the mission and values of the company. Our mission at the time was: "To create a world where anyone can belong anywhere." It makes little sense to just ask whether someone agrees with the mission; instead, we wanted to understand the person's thought processes. Relative to that mission, we would ask questions like: "Tell me about the last trip you took—how did you decide to go there, and how did you approach planning the trip?" We looked for signals that the candidate was interested in exploring cultures and living like a local, rather than just enjoying superficial travel experiences.

Were we only interested in adventurers? No. Let's say someone's idea of a great vacation was to go to Disney. That's fine. We would then ask: "Tell me what you did while you were there." If you ended up seeking out Mickey Mouse and Goofy so you could dance with them, that would be a plus. If the answer was that they bought the VIP pass that let them cut to the front of the line—not so much. We wanted to understand how people interacted with wherever they chose to go.

Keeping Your Feet to the Fire

Sometimes the culture worked by exposing cases where the values were not followed. For example, an important value was to "Be a host." We didn't mean you literally needed to turn your home into an Airbnb property; after all, some of our employees lived in studio apartments, had housemates, or their leases didn't permit "subletting." It was more about having the spirit of a host in terms of having empathy and consideration for others.

The stated values changed a bit over time, because we wanted them to be core values that our employees could remember, instead of just nice sounding statements in a file somewhere. Besides: "Be a host," another value was: "Be a cereal entrepreneur."[3] We wanted to preserve the mindset of being a scrappy startup, looking for opportunities, even when we were growing by thousands of employees across the globe. Another value was "Embrace the adventure," which was about having an open mindset and being a lifelong learner, given that we were pioneering new territories in the sharing economy.

Finally, there was: "Champion the mission." Hundreds of people applied for each of our openings. We therefore had the luxury of being very selective and used the core values interviewing as a way to be sure we could scale our culture. We didn't want people joining just to enhance their resume or because they wanted to get in on a possible equity windfall. We were looking for people who had a passion for connecting people through travel and for being authentic.

One of the most-loved aspects of working at Airbnb was how we created community around food. We were not like some of the legendary tech firms that hired Michelin chefs; instead, we had hardworking, down-to-earth employees who made three meals a day for us. They were considered the "hosts of the company" not only for the food, but through their considerate treatment of employees. Each meal would be inspired by an Airbnb listing in the many countries Airbnb operated in, so breakfast might be Spanish, lunch could be Canadian, and maybe dinner was Korean. It wasn't over-the-top fancy food; just authentic to the region.

---

[3] The wording is not a typo; it refers to an episode when the founders used a box of cereal to make a point with investors. All employees understood the reference.

I remember one time I was meeting with a visitor to Airbnb, and we were in the cafeteria. He asked whether we had a no laptop policy there. I said: "No; why do you ask?" He said that because it was so unusual to see everyone just engaging with each other and not hunched over laptops, working while eating. That was just the culture. We even encouraged employees to bring their families for dinner; not so employees would work longer hours, but just for the community aspect.

It was in the context of this culture and environment that a shockwave went through Airbnb when some billboard ads appeared all around San Francisco. People honestly thought that whoever bought the ad space was taking a swing at Airbnb—and they turned out to be ads created by Airbnb! The internal consternation reverberated for a while: *How could these ads have been approved by anyone who was aware of our values?* The executives responsible for the billboards stepped up and admitted that even though they had not seen the final product, that was no excuse. Procedures got adjusted, so this kind of messaging that was inconsistent with the values wouldn't happen again.

Another mechanism we established was a Core Values Council. It consisted of people chosen from across different levels and locations within the company. They all had been with Airbnb for a while, understood the values deeply, and had a passion for looking at decisions through the lens of those values. It wasn't just the founders or C-suite that upheld the values. The Council's opinions were sought for important aspects of the business, like acquisitions, layoffs, marketing campaigns (after the billboard affair), and strategic partnerships. They helped us to avoid certain other potentially embarrassing situations, for instance, when they pointed out that a certain celebrity endorser would not quite be a sterling example of our values.

The thing about building a culture where people feel like they count, they're listened to, and they co-create the organizations is that when they hold your feet to the fire, it hurts. It's absolutely the right thing to do, but it still can be painful for everyone. As painful as it is, the alternative is worse, where it's an attitude of: *Our job is to make policy and your job is to follow it. That's what you get paid for.*

This has been a long chapter because it's important to see how a whole variety of organizational outcomes can be driven by Employee

Experience Design. It's that linkage to many important outcomes that makes EXD such a valuable approach. For organizations that realize its power, EXD is how they get things done.

Chapter Summary

A core principle of EXD is that for it to be effective, it must be tied to organizational outcomes, serving as the "North Star" that provides a solid, explainable foundation.

EXD efforts directly support attracting the right talent, exemplified by Airbnb's #1 "Best Places to Work" ranking on Glassdoor, which resulted in many new hires through referrals.

It significantly contributes to employee retention, illustrated by Patagonia's policy changes like the four-day work week and the Traveling Companion Benefit for nursing mothers, which cost zero but dramatically reduced turnover and improved relationships.

EXD increases the chances that organizational initiatives will be successful by enlisting the help of those who will be affected, helping to prevent "dead on arrival" projects.

The chapter shows how EXD can lead to new product ideas (e.g., Febreze's accidental discovery) by creating conditions where employee creativity is unleashed.

EXD also improves the performance of teams by listening to and addressing their pain points, as seen with Guild's Recruiting Coordinators who became Candidate Experience Specialists and received an energy boost at no cost.

Finally, EXD helps create a culture that "self-corrects," demonstrated by Airbnb's Ground Control and core values interview process, which supported alignment with the mission and values as the company scaled.

4

A Conversation with Beth Grous

The Impact of Trust and Humanity, and the Courage of Everyday Leaders

Background

Dean, Beth, and I (Mark) met when we were on the HRPS Advisory Board (part of the Society for Human Resources Professionals Association, focused on HR Execs). We completely bonded as our approach to HR was employee-centric and more inclusive of their voices than what you find with traditional HR leaders.

Beth was at TripAdvisor when I was at Airbnb, so we had an industry in common. Years ago, we both dabbled in what we now call Employee Experience. We learned from each other about ways we leveraged our people, culture, and travel into our workplaces, and how we worked with employees to identify priorities and design solutions. We also took our show on the road, sharing these insights at many conferences. You're going to love Beth's stories and insights.

Could you please tell us a little about where you are now?

I'm the Chief People Officer at Generate:Biomedicines. We're pioneering what we call "generative biology"; it's a revolutionary approach to drug development. We do this by combining machine learning, automated experimentation, and science to build novel proteins. Our goal is to generate medicines to treat humanity's most intractable diseases. It's an exciting company filled with exceptionally smart and passionate people.

I joined Generate because I was inspired by the mission of the company and really intrigued by the technology, when AI was not part of the lexicon the way it is today. In fact, I got the offer the same month that ChatGPT was introduced to the world. It's proven to be a great choice to be here. Now we're a 300-ish-person company, and I've found there's a lot of innovation that we can drive, on both the science and Employee Experience side.

What were your jobs before Generate:Biomedicines?

For seven and a half years, I was the Chief People Officer at Tripadvisor. I joined in 2015 as the first senior HR leader, even though the company was 15 years old. They had a very open and creative leadership team. It still felt a lot like a startup, though it was a 2,700-person company when I joined the organization.

Before that, I was an SVP of HR at Nuance, which was subsequently acquired by Microsoft. Prior to that, I spent more than a decade at Genzyme, the rare-disease-focused biotech acquired by Sanofi in 2011. I've also been in consumer product and services companies, among other industries. The last couple of decades of my career have been focused exclusively on tech and biotech, working in companies where the product was something that I believed in, where the values of the company resonated with me, and where I thought there was an opportunity to build and to make an impact on both the people and business strategies.

When were you first exposed to the concept of EX, even if it wasn't called that initially?

Although creating great experiences for employees has always been part of how I worked, my first "formal" exposure was Tripadvisor, although until

I met Mark and Dean, I wasn't calling it EX. Rather, it was about continuously asking: "How do we work more collaboratively with our people to create a work experience that inspires and enables them to bring their best self to work every day?"

An interesting thing about Tripadvisor is that it's a business that reviews hotels, experiences, and restaurants based on the view of the user. Let's say you're a hotel and you're getting these very individual, unvarnished reviews. You can decide to respond to them and to engage with the feedback to improve; by doing so, travelers understand that management is listening, reacting, and responding, including saying thank you for a positive review. Or as a hotelier, you may choose to ignore any negative or constructive feedback, and in doing so, people will assume the reviewers were right, and this isn't a great place to stay. Around the time I joined, there was a clear intuition in the organization that, hey, maybe we should run HR the same way—actively engaging with our "customers" (in this case, employees), by asking questions, listening, and responding.

HR had been a somewhat administrative and largely recruiting-oriented function before I arrived. Tripadvisor's CEO and co-founder is a wonderful, innovative leader, Steve Kaufer. When I was interviewing with him, Steve described the customer review process. He then said that we should change HR, working with our employees in the same way that we work with our hoteliers and our restaurateurs: Understand the experience the employee is having, get that feedback, and then react to it. That really aligned with my personal philosophy.

Another thing that impressed me when I was interviewing with Tripadvisor was the new headquarters that was purpose-built to mirror the experience of a traveler. In fact, the person running the facilities team, Matt Gabree, was not a facilities expert, but a hospitality leader and culinary school graduate hired from W Hotels. Matt knew that when you go into a well-run hotel, the whole experience is planned to optimize your stay and elevate your impression of the property—everything from the scent that gets piped in at the front desk; to the person who greets you; how you get from the lobby to your room; and all the things that make your stay easy, seamless, and memorable. There are lessons in there for a work environment: If we want to encourage things like collaboration and co-creation, we should have workspaces that are intentionally designed to make work easier for our employees.

> On the very rare occasions when there was a misstep, we managed those outliers. It's freedom within a framework.

With that in mind, the building was designed to foster collaboration. We had two pubs where people could gather, and these pubs had alcohol on tap 24/7. I'm here to tell you that no one ever abused that, because we conveyed trust to our employees that they would act responsibly and use common sense. In this and in all things, we told them what we expected. We assumed that if you were part of our team, we could trust that you had good judgment and the intuition to make the right choices the vast majority of the time. On the very rare occasions when there was a misstep, we managed those outliers. It's freedom within a framework.

In contrast, I think many companies and traditional HR teams orient themselves around risk management and compliance. What if we get sued, and how do we manage the day-to-day life here to prevent that? If there's a one-in-a-million chance that we end up in court, we can pull out our 800-page employee manual and point to page 674 and say, "Aha! This is where we told the person they couldn't do that!" I think that's a totally unnecessary way to manage.

You ended up with several areas reporting to you at Tripadvisor, right?

Yes. Within the first few months, facilities came to report to me. We called it "Office Experience." I also led the charitable foundation and our philanthropic arm, because that was a very big part of our culture. We put a lot of emphasis on volunteerism and the practice of giving back. The mission of our foundation was to help displaced populations like refugees and others who are what you might call "travelers not by choice."

What are some misconceptions about EX?

A common one is that it's all about lots of expensive benefits and pretty things—and it's actually not that. I mean, some companies do have expensive benefits and pretty things, but that's not equivalent to EX. I look at EX as a very deliberate creation and purposeful alignment of your culture and your business strategy, engaging employees in that co-creation process. It's how we deliberately design the employee experience, from pre-hire all the way through to our alumni programs, and how we amplify business outcomes by doing so. That's what I spent seven and a half years there doing.

Not everything we did worked. For example, we had this beautiful purpose-built building for collaboration, but we came to realize that whole spaces were not being used. So, we asked people what they wanted and ended up redesigning those spaces to meet the needs of our teams.

There was another example of "less is more." Before I started at Tripadvisor, an outside events firm was hired to help plan our first holiday party in the new HQ. The plans they delivered were truly over-the-top with ice rinks, ice sculptures, professional skaters, and other stuff. That was the "design for them" approach. We reworked the scope of that first party not to include any of those things. When we asked people what was the most important thing they wanted for the next holiday event, we learned it was simply to be in community with each other. They wanted an event that reflected the fact that we were a global organization and not just in the United States. They wanted to spend time with colleagues, to give back, and to celebrate the year that had just ended. All of those things can be accomplished in a much more cost-effective way, and we did that in later years, incorporating things like charitable auctions and fun (and often low or no cost) themes.

It's tempting to want to do over-the-top things, but I don't know a single company out there that's got infinite resources and isn't thinking: *How do we spend our cash wisely and get a return on this investment?*

It sounds like Airbnb, Tripadvisor, and Patagonia have something in common in that Legal didn't take over and demand that all the edge cases had to be planned for. What would you say to someone reading this who's thinking: *My organization is different. Our legal department doesn't get the concept of "freedom within a framework" as you called it.* **What would be your advice?**

I would say a couple of things. First, there is a real ROI on EX. This isn't just a bunch of freewheeling HR folks wanting to do crazy, legally risky things. Start by defining what the problem is that you want to solve: Is it to create a great experience that measurably drives engagement, retention, innovation, and business results? Or are you trying to predict the edge case rules violation that you might encounter 10 years down the road and protect for it now?

> *There is a real ROI on EX. This isn't just a bunch of freewheeling HR folks wanting to do crazy, legally risky things.*

Some conservative attorneys (and frankly, some HR traditionalists; it's not just the lawyers) would rather build giant policy structures in the futile attempt to anticipate every edge case, rather than deal with these cases if they infrequently occur.

I do think you need a CEO who is practical. Listen, I've been doing HR for a long time. There's barely a problem that you can't solve—long before you need to think about litigation—with a little bit of work. Part of it is just treating people fairly. How do you minimize employment litigation? It's when people walk away feeling respected and heard; when they understand the decisions, and they've been treated fairly. It's not because they signed a hefty policy manual when they started with the company five years ago—a manual that they probably never read, but just scrolled down to the bottom and clicked.

My advice to HR folks who feel like they're running up against a legal wall is just to keep asking, "What could we do to make this work? How much risk are we really talking about? Is the risk so outweighed by the reward and by the business impact?"

Our general counsels at Tripadvisor and at Generate are pretty progressive. They're like: "Beth, I trust you. I don't need to micromanage this. You've got this. You've been doing it for a long time." We have a lot of respect and affection for each other, and we recognize that we're here to solve the same set of business problems together. By the way, your attorneys are employees, too, and they want to be beneficiaries of the same awesome EX.

We just discussed working with Legal. Sometimes a CFO has concerns along the lines of: "If we co-design with employees, it'll end up costing us a fortune." Have you found that to be the case, or have you come across other obstacles to implementing EX?

The tone gets set at the top, and the CEO will select for people who are culturally on the same wavelength. When organizations run up against a CFO, there are two things I'd say. First, how do you articulate the business value of what you're doing?

Some things in EX may not have business value. For example, when I started at Tripadvisor, one thing we offered on site was manicures. Remember this was circa 2015 in the tech industry: The practice had been to just throw every benefit at people because that's what you did.

By involving employees in the discussion, we learned that manicures were nice to have, but their availability every Wednesday was not what attracted and retained our employees, nor did it make them more collaborative or innovative. We took those savings and invested in other things that were more in line with our values.

For example, we spent a lot of money on food; that aligned with our value of bringing people together to break bread and experience cuisines from around the world. We had a very multicultural cafeteria, which was a direct reflection of the business that we were in. This choice deepened employee engagement and connection, and it was the right business choice for us to make.

The CEO totally got that, even though sometimes he would twitch at the cost. Then again, he would be the first one to say that he could stand by the salad bar at 12:15 on any day of the week, talk to 15 people, and get quick wins. There's real value in that. So, to the extent you can, it is important to quantify the business value and become very selective about investments that deliver a meaningful return.

Also, not all EX has to cost money: Talking with people, listening to their ideas, and creating with them is free. When you choose to say no to an employee request or suggestion, it's important to explain to people the reason. It may be a compliance, regulatory, or financial reason, or something else. Most employees I find are pretty darn reasonable when you treat them like adults.

> *When you choose to say no to an employee request or suggestion, it's important to explain to people the reason.*

This reminds me of another point: A lot of old-style buildings have the executive suite behind glass, in the corner or on another floor. This is a sure way to signal to your workforce that executives are intentionally inaccessible. Put your offices closer to people. Walk around more, eat in the cafeteria, say hello to people on the elevator, and introduce yourself. It's not that hard. Little actions truly go a long way.

I'll tell you a funny Tripadvisor story. We had hundreds of Glassdoor reviews. After I started, we began to respond to them. After all, we told our hoteliers that when someone leaves you a review—particularly if it's negative—engage with that content and show people that you're listening.

With that "hotelier approach" in mind, I started responding on Glassdoor. When someone identified themselves as a former employee, I would say, "Hey, you know how to get in touch with me; I would love to talk to you." If someone was a current employee, I'd ask them to send me a Slack message so we could meet and talk. Doing so shows that I'm reading your comment, and I'm genuinely interested in your opinion.

Within the first two weeks of doing this, I received a meeting invite from someone in Singapore. I had never met them and didn't know what it was about, but I accepted. It was eight or nine o'clock at night. And they said, "Hi, I'm the person that wrote that Glassdoor review. I can't believe that you responded and are happy to talk." We had a great conversation, and I walked away with actionable things to bring to my team. After doing this sort of thing for a while, I saw a review on Glassdoor. It's probably still there. It said: "I know when I write this review, Beth is going to say, if you have a question, come talk to me. So, I just want everyone to know, I've already talked to her about all the things that I'm writing in this note, and she's acted on one already." It was such a big win. The more you can listen, act, and respond, it drives this virtuous cycle, and all of that is free.

How do you measure the success of EX?

Some of it is measurable, and some of it isn't a direct cause-and-effect situation. We send surveys to our candidates and ask about their experience in the interview process. We then use that input to improve the process. Do I know that a specific improvement was the only factor that drove my acceptance rate on offers from 91 percent to 93 percent? No, but what I do know is that we had very high acceptance rates on offers, because we continuously tuned the engine in real time.

If you think after you spend money on a beautiful cafeteria or on collaboration spaces that you're going to get a specific ROI—it's squishier than that. It's the whole Employee Value Proposition. But there are metrics like, "Would you refer this place to a friend?" or "Are there changes to our workplace you would suggest that can enhance collaboration?"

If you run an organization where managers feel empowered to create a great work environment for their people within a framework—and that's how you're defining employee experience—then of course, your employee productivity and innovation will be better than if they don't. That's just common sense.

Also, you have to be careful about jumping to conclusions with some measurements. In one employee survey, one of the lowest-scoring things was about physical space. That result could drive all sorts of expensive remedies, but the first thing we did was ask employees: "What led you to score it this low, and how do we fix this for you?" In a very open floor plan, people suggested a simple solution: They said we didn't need to do anything with the floor plan, but could we pipe in some white noise, so they can concentrate better? That's so easy, and it helped us avoid a set of capital improvements that were not necessary.

What do you find is the hardest thing to convince people of who aren't yet on board?

EX must be intentional. There is a difference between traditional HR and having an employee experience foundation. Like anything worth doing, you have to be committed to it. You can't do things the old way, add in free lunch, and conclude, "We're done." It does require a change in mindset from: *We are HR; we know it all and we're going to roll things out.* Instead, it's about asking: "What are some things that would enhance your productivity? How do we make this a better place to work? What would make you unreservedly recommend this place to a friend to come work here?" On both the teams at Tripadvisor and at Generate—where we call our team People & Culture—our mantra is: "We do things *for* and *with* our employees, not *to* them." I stole that phrase from you, Mark, and it really captures the philosophy, and guides our actions.

EX is a business strategy, first and foremost. It is not a bunch of far-out HR people who decide that they want to work differently. This is explicitly about driving business outcomes by having a more highly engaged, highly collaborative, innovative workforce who really understand and buy into the strategy of your company. EX is the intentional amplification and reflection of culture and strategy, and this alignment supports people working in the highest impact way.

> *This is explicitly about driving business outcomes by having a more highly engaged, highly collaborative, innovative workforce who really understand and buy into the strategy of your company.*

Do you think there is an issue with the term "HR"?

HR isn't necessarily a bad term, but it has a lot of baggage that sometimes does more harm than good. Recently, I was talking with a senior leader and he said, "I had horrific experiences with HR at my prior company." It was one of the large pharmaceutical companies, and I asked why it was so horrific. He described it as very traditional HR, with an emphasis on command and control, a lot of saying no, here's the policy, you can't do that, and so on. I explained that our team's goal was to support him to be more expansive in his leadership and not more restrictive. EX helps organizations to be more expansive.

HR gets such a bad rap. How often have you heard someone say, "I'm going to get sent to HR" as the worst form of punishment? The reputation reflects how teams choose to act. I think many people don't realize that you actually have agency to reinvent this thing.

Let's say somebody picks up this book who isn't at the C-suite level—not a senior person at all—but is absolutely lit up with the possibilities. What would you advise that person to do who doesn't have a lot of authority in the organization to get it going there?

First act locally, within your own team. Ask people for feedback, and explicitly for what's working and what is not. Then have the humility to listen with curiosity and respond. Be willing to listen twice as closely to the hard stuff, and to double down twice as much on fixing the hard stuff.

I guarantee you that the leader who asks their team, "How do we make this place somewhere that you're happy to come to every day, where you feel like you're doing the best work of your life?"—that leader will have higher productivity and lower attrition on their team. They'll probably promote more people into positions inside the organization.

The really excellent leaders trying to create a great experience for their team have the attitude of *let's not break the stuff that you told us we're doing well, but let's really focus on fixing the stuff where there's an opportunity*. It should be viewed as an opportunity and not a criticism. Every leader can create great experiences for their team within almost any organization, and despite any set of constraints they have. They should try to get the backing of their manager and their manager's manager for doing that.

I realize it's very hard to swim upstream. Sometimes it's true that you look around and think, *I want to work differently*, but the organization's culture makes that difficult to impossible, despite your best efforts. Maybe it's not the place where you should be working, and you can find a place where you have a different kind of impact.

Most innovation doesn't happen in the C-suite, just like scientific discovery does not happen in the C-suite—it happens at the lab bench, or in small teams thinking around a whiteboard or over a meal. It takes someone with curiosity to think, *What can I do with this thing?*

I've been fortunate with my last two CEOs. They are both incredibly transparent, humble, and curious, and really believe in the power of teams. They recognize that they do not have all the answers, and that collective decision-making is so much better than the top-down way. Their view of HR is as a business function that enables us to execute on our strategies through people and talent.

Not all CEOs think that way. I've been in companies where the CEO thought he had all the answers. The best CEOs understand that companies are built on people. You need to plan and have strategies to get the best alchemy out of the teams you have, and figure out interesting ways to do that.

When my oldest daughter, Jennifer, was recently entering the workforce, my advice was to pick the best boss that she could find—someone who would champion her ideas, give her feedback, and expose her to lots of things and not put her in a box. For early career talent, that's actually more important than the work you're doing.

One thing that I'll just leave you with is that in my current job and other jobs—whether it's in a reporting structure or not—the synergy between legal, finance, comms, facilities, and HR has to come together for EX. And it doesn't have to be through hardline reporting to one person. If that won't happen in your organization, then don't be deterred. Figure out how you get stuff done through influence.

There's so much room for EX. We're thinking about extending this into pre-hire and also when you hit the inevitable time where you've got to do a downsizing or layoff, how do you think about EX in that context as well. I've got a lot of views on that. EX extends beyond the employment experience: How you treat people when they're in the candidate pipeline and not hired, or when they are off boarding can be as important as how you treated them when they worked for you.

Thanks for taking the time to share your long history with EX, Beth, and your interesting perspectives!

You're very welcome.

Chapter Summary

Beth emphasizes conveying trust and promoting "freedom within a framework," contrasting this with traditional HR's focus on risk management and compliance.

She clarifies that EXD is not about expensive benefits but the deliberate co-creation of culture and business strategy with employees, from pre-hire to alumni programs.

She discusses overcoming resistance from Legal and CFOs by articulating the clear ROI of EXD and involving employees in benefit decisions to ensure wise spending and business value.

Beth highlights the importance of senior leaders being visible, accessible, and responsive (for example, responding to Glassdoor reviews) to build trust and demonstrate listening.

She asserts that EXD is fundamentally a business strategy that drives outcomes like an engaged, collaborative, and innovative workforce, rather than being "freewheeling HR."

Beth advises individuals without C-suite authority to act locally within their own teams, asking for feedback with humility and curiosity, because this will lead to higher productivity and lower attrition.

PART II | Prepare

5

Mindsets

Seven Mindsets for Employee Experience Design

We live in an age of push-button convenience. We push a button to start our car or to heat up a meal. We make a few clicks to write a resume or "compose" an original song on AI. There seems to be no end to what we can do with a button, click, or swipe.

We have some good news and bad news for you. First, the bad: There are no buttons you can press or AI prompts to write that will do the heavy lifting when designing an effective employee experience. This brings us to the good news: Because you will be rolling up your sleeves to design the employee experience with your organization, it will be custom-tailored to whatever makes your situation unique.

Peter Drucker, the famous management consultant, said: "Only three things happen naturally in organizations: Friction, confusion, and underperformance. Everything else requires leadership."[1]

---

[1] Drucker, Peter. *The Effective Executive*. Saint Louis: Routledge, 2018.

The leadership we'll discuss in this chapter involves first doing things differently from the well-worn path that many initiatives follow; then it's about combining certain elements of EXD in a way that works for your organization.

The Path of Least Resistance

Above, we referred to the "well-worn path." People take that path, for example, when they're under pressure to implement a new policy. They may have been reminded that "time is money" and that the deadline is somewhere around "yesterday." Here's what that project looks like when done the conventional way:

1. We often start with "best practices." We're not sure how they became written that way, but at least there's comfort in knowing that someone ranked them as "best."
2. For the details, we might also cut and paste or piggyback heavily on what other organizations have delivered, even if those organizations bear little resemblance to ours.
3. We end up spending a LOT of time on the policy, trying to anticipate all the "edge cases" where someone can abuse the system, and there are a lot of them.
4. We get someone to wordsmith the material above into the style we use for our other policies.
5. We run it by Legal, which complicates the language, but hey, that's what they usually do.
6. We present the policy to the leadership group for sign-off.
7. There was no time for employee involvement and besides, they're not experts on the policy we need to announce.
8. We roll out the policy with employees. We may or may not ask for feedback and hope there isn't any, because we've already gotten approval for it as is.
9. The policy gets buried in the policy section of the handbook and filed away until someone says it needs updating.

Kind of a typical process, right? The problem: It generates typical results: Now a policy exists, which seems like progress. But the policy likely does not further any organizational goals of the type we discussed in Chapter 3, like aiding in recruiting or retention, improving team performance, and so on.

In this chapter, we'll discuss in some depth the different approach that EXD takes to create a policy. Let's summarize how it works:

1. We don't start with best practices, but instead we start with "Why." We take the time to get real clarity on the purpose. We'll see later how this can completely change the final policy product.
2. We replace the effort to search for examples and best practices with instead searching for the current situation that exists among our employees, managers, and leaders.
3. We ask those groups to help us understand what a successful policy might look like.
4. We work with Legal, but strive to have the policy be written in plain language that still meets legal requirements. (By the way, it can be done.)
5. We apply several other tests, as you will hear, to make sure the policy is as effective as possible.
6. When we roll out the policy, there's no guessing about "buy in" because people are already "bought in."
7. We don't consider the policy to be "done" because we expect iterations and are ready to modify or even delete the policy as circumstances warrant.

This different approach might take less time or in some cases even more time than the old approach. What's significantly different is the policy enhances the employee experience while meeting organization objectives. Of course, policy development is not the only use for EXD; we just wanted you to see the contrast at a high level.

So how exactly do we go from the *status quo* to having something that contributes to a great employee experience?

Employee Value Proposition

In Chapter 2, we defined some key terms like EX and EXD. Now let's add an important one to the mix: Employee Value Proposition. To define it succinctly:

> The Employee Value Proposition is everything an organization offers in exchange for the skills, knowledge, and experience that employees bring to work.

It's a simply stated concept, but it has a lot of component parts, depending on the organization. It's a mixture of the following:

- **Purpose.** Some organizations have such a clear and necessary purpose for existing that this element alone can inspire and attract people to work there. The opposite can be oppressive: After I (Mark) became a lawyer, I worked at a regional consumer electronics company. The way the job was described to me, my role was to catch people doing something wrong. They prioritized surveillance and punitive measures. Ugh. I felt like an imposter because I had become a lawyer in order to help people.
- **Brand.** A great example of this is where I (Dean) worked: Patagonia. Not only were we known the world over, but we were proud of what the brand represented: Creating the best possible products while energetically working to save the environment.
- **Work environment.** I (Mark) and many others put an enormous effort into making Airbnb a great environment in which to work. You sometimes hear about bosses ordering their employees back to working in person. We had very strategic and talented architects on the team, who designed incredibly beautiful and inspiring work spaces. Even so, in some cases, we co-designed our workplaces with our employees. With their input, we had the comfort of home with the functionality of an office. Our employees not only co-designed the functional space, but also chose listings from around the world; then they decorated meeting rooms to reflect our hosts' homes—a living room, dining room, or kitchen. We ended up with most people coming to the office because

they wanted to, not because they had to. It was a place of community and, as you heard earlier, food was at the center of bringing people together in our cafes. Check out this link that highlighted the co-creation where we won a Cannes Design Award.
- **Physical workspace.** This is different from the general work environment. When I (Dean) joined Patagonia, to say that they had disdain for HR would be putting it mildly. We were housed at the edge of the Patagonia campus—in an old double-wide trailer. (We later turned that perception around, and by the time I left, more than eight years later, we were in the center of campus at a building nicknamed "the Crystal Palace" with its fancy atrium.)
- **Pay.** Of course, this is a huge factor for many employees across the globe. In fact, we all have heard about or worked in places where pay was the only reason to drag ourselves to work and endure the day.
- **Benefits.** We talked about Patagonia's Traveling Companion Benefit in Chapter 3. Another benefit that became a recruiting magnet was at Airbnb, where employees got $1,000 per year in travel vouchers to stay in Airbnb listings anywhere. Besides being a great and unusual benefit, it furthered our business goal of having employees connect more with hosts worldwide and bring that knowledge back to the workplace. Talk about unusual benefits: If you were arrested while peaceably protesting for an environmental cause, Patagonia would pay your bail, and it would be considered paid time off. They also had 35 internships where you could go anywhere in the world to save something.
- **Team.** This is such a huge factor in organizations, because it defines so much of your work life. Are you left to fend for yourself with no mentor? Or are you part of a team that might work insane hours but you're with fabulous people and have clear goals? The Apple Macintosh team was like that: They worked like dogs but were creating a product that changed the face of personal computing.
- **Policies.** As we've discussed, well-crafted policies can help people to feel like they've been heard, and the opposite is all too common.
- **Processes.** When processes are poor or absent, work becomes saturated with frustration. In *Competing Against Time*, an excellent book about time-based competition, the authors talk about research that

it's typical in manufacturing for a product to be actually worked on only 0.05 percent to 5 percent of the time. In other words, it's sitting and waiting, between 95 percent and 99.95 percent of the time.[2] Conversely, it's a pleasure when teams have processes that get the work done smoothly and effectively.

- **Programs offered.** These might be opportunities to rotate between departments, learn more skills, and advance in the organization. It could also be a mentoring arrangement where an experienced person can meet on company time to "pay it forward" and bring along a younger employee in terms of advice and problem solving.
- **Opportunities to volunteer.** This was a major focus at Gap Inc. The Fischer family (founders) encouraged employees to volunteer, and the top volunteers were chosen to go on "volunteer vacations" to New Orleans after Hurricane Katrina and to Guatemala to build housing.

At each Airbnb office worldwide, we had social impact champions, because we incorporated social impact into onboarding, years-of-service awards, and holiday gatherings. We partnered with nonprofits to provide meaningful volunteer opportunities. In many cases, we volunteered alongside our hosts at nonprofits that were meaningful to them in their communities.

All offices would regularly engage in community service in their local areas, and we provided all our employees up to four hours per month of paid time to volunteer. All of this supported the Airbnb brand, but more importantly it was meaningful for the people who passed our culture interviews and were looking for causes greater than taking home a paycheck.

Patagonia paid for an eight-week environmental internship for any employee, anywhere in the world, which was reviewed, approved, and run by a volunteer employee council. The company also 100 percent matched all nonprofit contributions up to a specific amount.

---

[2] Stalk, George, and Thomas M. Hout. *Competing Against Time: How Time-based Competition Is Reshaping Global Markets.* New York: Free Press etc., 1990, pp 76–7.

Just as your organization has an Employee Experience, whether you like it or not—you also have an Employee Value Proposition. For a lot of employees worldwide, the proposition often looks pretty dismal:

- "I need to work here because of the health benefits package."
- "It's the only job I could find where I can get there on public transportation; my wife also works and needs the car."
- "I hate everything about this Wall Street job, except for the possibility that I can trade a few years of my life and then move up the ladder."

Of the three acronyms—EX, EXD, and EVP—only Employee Experience Design is optional. As we've mentioned, its rarity gives it the power to transform your organization well beyond what your competitors have going for them. It's also the shortest path to improving your Employee Value Proposition.

Seven Essential EXD Mindsets

We don't know what your musical tastes run to, but you may have heard of Mickey Hart. He was a drummer for The Grateful Dead. Mickey talked about how he could not walk down the street in any city without hearing amazing rhythms that inspired his music. He said: "Life is about rhythm. We vibrate, our hearts are pumping blood, we are a rhythm machine, that's what we are."[3]

We bring him up because Mickey is a great example of mindset. Mickey doesn't just play a song and then stop thinking of music when he's not performing. It's just a part of him. He doesn't have to work at hearing rhythms everywhere.

In a sense, that can happen with Employee Experience Design. You get accustomed to looking at organizational projects and challenges through the lens of EXD. With time, your knee-jerk reaction becomes: "Let's involve employees in the design of that new space" or whatever is the project.

---

[3] https://www.elephantdrums.co.uk/blog/guides-and-resources/drumming-quotes-famous-drummers/

Let's look at some fundamental mindset principles that together form the EXD approach.

1. **Find mutual value.** The place of mutual value is finding solutions that are great for both employees and the organization. As we discussed earlier in this chapter, we wanted to design some new meeting rooms at Airbnb. The usual approach would have been to hire a design firm. Instead, we asked employees to co-create them. What a win-win: The company saved money, the spaces were beautiful and succeeded in furthering our value of making connections, and employees could be justifiably proud of their work.
2. **Just start small.** We all have suffered on projects that exhibited "scope creep": one maybe good idea glommed on to the next idea until the sum of the parts ... ground to a halt, even just during the planning phase. One indication of this is when projects stay on the list from one strategic planning session to the next. No one wants to kill the project, and no one's willing to get moving with it, either.

> *"Will gathering more information make it easier to make decisions?" Often, the answer is yes.*

The Romans had a good phrase for the antidote: *Festina Lente* or "Make haste slowly." We interpret that to mean just get started, even if it's at a slow pace. When you're part of this kind of analysis paralysis, it's helpful to ask: "Will gathering more information make it easier to make decisions?" Often, the answer is yes. The initial action—getting more data—can make the later action of making a decision easier.

3. **Find the Why.** This is such an important mindset. In some circles this is called a "Root-Cause Analysis." Here's an example: My (Samantha's) friend was tasked with finding a better Applicant Tracking System ("ATS") because managers were not booking many interviews with candidates. My friend had a design background, and that made him stop and instead do some quick discovery. (You will hear much more about discovery later.) He wanted to understand their experience and the reasons behind the lack of interview bookings.

What he found was that the real underlying problem—the Why—was not the interview booking technology. Instead, managers weren't booking interviews because they perceived the caliber of the candidates being sourced as poor. If he had found the best ATS on the planet, it would not have addressed the fundamental issue of candidate quality. Finding the underlying issue avoided a lot of misspent effort and money.

Another element in this principle is to listen like a detective. It means not being that person who's not really listening; instead, the person is merely waiting to talk again. Spending more time listening is time well spent.

4. **Design with, not for.** We've mentioned this already, but consider the following: When we're not at work, we have consumer-grade expectations. As consumers, we've come to expect some amazing things: Today's phones have 5,000 times faster computing speed than the Cray-2 supercomputer, costing millions in 1985.[4] We now expect products we order to arrive the next day and are not too surprised anymore when they arrive in a few hours. Every photo we've taken for decades is retrievable in seconds, and even categorized by AI.

Then we arrive at our desks at work. We struggle to find last year's presentation so we can update it. The ancient fluorescent lighting is literally triggering migraines in a large percentage of employees, but fixing that is not even on the horizon. The company suffers from bad ratings on Trustpilot and Google, despite spending a fortune on R&D.

It's these contrasts that employees can help with. People on the front lines in the call center know that customers gripe continuously about packaging issues: Leaking product and dented product. Labels that are driving customers nuts. Why? Because they can't be cleanly removed. So the first experience customers have with the gorgeous new phone case we shipped is this unsightly half-removed label that must now be scratched off. Labels don't get elevated to the attention of the highly paid designers, but the front-line folks hear about them all day long.

---

[4] https://blog.adobe.com/en/publish/2022/11/08/fast-forward-comparing-1980s-supercomputer-to-modern-smartphone

As for the migraines: A third of migraine attacks occur on workdays and two-thirds of these result in substantial productivity losses. Three times as many women experience them as men.[5] It's a safe bet that if more spaces were designed *with* employees—not *for* them—some of these people would be absolutely delighted to participate in finding solutions. They can be inexpensive too, like monitor filters that block blue light and finding spaces lit more by daylight than by fluorescent light for people who endure migraines. Imagine the word-of-mouth reputational benefit that would come from employees on Glassdoor or social media who finally found an employer that worked with them to reduce their daily debilitating headaches. Patagonia had a "no fragrances" policy designed by employees whose migraines were triggered by powerful scents.

5. **Test and iterate.** Silicon Valley has two great concepts that any organization can use. The first is "Minimum Viable Product" or "MVP." We may have lofty plans for the next software app, but it's so revolutionary that we don't know how it will be received. With the MVP concept, what is the bare minimum we must deliver in order to get feedback from users?

That brings us to the second concept: "You don't learn until you ship." Only when you get that app out the door and into the hands of users will you find out if it's brilliant, OK, or terrible. These concepts can just as easily be used in a nonprofit that's building clean, basic cinderblock housing in Haiti: How quickly can we build the simplest iteration of our housing concept? That will allow us to "ship" it and get the vital feedback we need to do Version 2.0.

"Here's our new guide. We're not sure that we have it exactly right; what do you think?"

Here's a pro tip to use when gathering feedback from users. Let's say you have a new guide for something and you're collecting early feedback. If you ask users: "Here's our new guide; what do you think?" you might get some different answers, but they'll be biased in the positive direction. Most people

---
[5] https://pmc.ncbi.nlm.nih.gov/articles/PMC8061063/

don't want to offend. If instead you say: "Here's our new guide. We're not sure that we have it exactly right; what do you think?" Now you have given them permission to say either: "No, this is good stuff!" or "You're right; I'm confused by what you say here."

6. **Make it BASIC.** I (Samantha) use this acronym all the time in my consulting work with organizations. Let's say you've convened a group of people from multiple levels in your organization to craft a new policy about expense reimbursements. It's easy to get way deep into the weeds and design something that covers every conceivable situation, but you don't want it to be too complex to be explained and administered.

I've found it useful to see if the new policy meets the BASIC test:

- **Beautiful:** Just as the best consumer products and services put a premium on good design, so should employee-facing systems, processes, and environments. It need not be extravagant, but instead just thoughtful and well-executed.
- **Accessible:** Can employees access the information or tool easily and find what they're looking for quickly and intuitively?
- **Simple:** Have we distilled this policy to the fewest points possible, and left the "edge cases" to be handled separately? Also, is the end product clean and uncluttered?
- **Intuitive:** Can employees use common sense and easily access the systems or follow the processes without extensive training?
- **Consistent:** Just as consumers expect consistency from their favorite brands, does this product or service seamlessly fit with our other policies and technology?

We've found that most employee experiences do not meet even one or two of these criteria, never mind all five. That's good news, because it means there's opportunity everywhere to improve EX at your organization.

7. **Be kind.** This sounds like obvious advice, but it has several implications for EXD. It's easy to be kind to people we already know and like,

but the design process we're discussing means digging deeply into the thoughts and ideas of people who may not have been asked for their opinions much before. The following is worth keeping in mind:

Take a non judgmental approach when having conversations because people may be coming from very different viewpoints.

Show empathy and try to see how people might have reached the perspective they have.

Avoid confirmation bias. Look to understand and not to validate the approach we would prefer.

Expect emotions. When people realize they're being asked to give their actual feelings about something, it can result in the dam overflowing, so to speak. That's a good thing because we're getting beyond window dressing to the real deal, but it can also be emotional for everyone involved.

Look after people. Employees may regret being honest right after doing so, because they didn't expect to go that far. It's important to support their honesty, or else you won't be able to elicit it again down the road.

It's easier to list a set of mindsets than it is to follow them, especially when they've not all been the way most organizations have traditionally done things. At the end of this book is a page that describes how you can get additional useful materials. There, you can request an email with an attachment of all these mindsets arranged on one page for easy reference.

Now that you have the mindsets necessary for effective Employee Experience Design, it's time to talk about the key processes at your disposal.

Chapter Summary

Effective EXD isn't the traditional policy development approach (top-down, focused on anticipating edge cases, often without employee involvement). Instead, EXD starts with "why" and designs with employees.

The Employee Value Proposition (EVP) is everything an organization offers in exchange for employee skills. It includes elements like purpose; brand; work environment; pay; benefits; team; policies; processes; programs; and volunteer opportunities.

Mindsets

Seven mindsets are fundamental to EXD:

1. Find mutual value (win-win for employees and organization).
2. Just start small (avoid analysis paralysis).
3. Find the Why (root-cause analysis, listen like a detective).
4. Design with, not for (leverage front-line insights, address pain points).
5. Iterate (create a Minimum Viable Product; you don't learn until you ship; invite honest feedback).
6. Make it BASIC (Beautiful, Accessible, Simple, Intuitive, Consistent).
7. Be kind (non judgmental, empathetic, avoid confirmation bias, support honesty).

6 | A Conversation with Kirsty Lloyd

How Empathy and Feedback Became Cultural Anchors at Scale

Background

I (Samantha) met Kirsty when she joined EX Design School, and I was immediately impressed by her pragmatism and deep commitment to people. With a strong commercial and operations background, Kirsty brought a grounded perspective, and when her company, Haka House, faced major disruption, she leaned into the challenge with openness and grit.

What really stood out was how closely she listened to her team at Haka, and the impact of that was evident. Kirsty, as Head of People, needed to generate buy-in and influence across the leadership group. She was genuinely surprised by how powerful this design-led approach could be, both in how it felt to work this way and the results it created. Kirsty shares her experience with honesty and vulnerability, and I know you'll take a lot from hearing her story.

Please tell us a little about your background, the main roles you've had, and where you are now.

I've had a fairly varied career, but most of my leadership roles have been in hospitality and tourism. I was head of the commercial side at Jucy Rentals, which is a large tourism business here in New Zealand. We were also in the US, Canada, and Australia at the time. We booked cars, campervans, hotels, and cruises.

Then COVID came along. It was pretty rocky and I wasn't made redundant, but I did decide halfway through that it was time for me to move to a different business. I'd been through the growth of the business, it was sold, and it was time for me to let somebody else drive the passion.

> *I came in as the operations manager in the middle of COVID. Three weeks later, the General Manager left, and I became GM. Five days after that, we went into a 110-day lockdown.*

When I came to Haka House Hostels, it was a step down in role, but it was also a great fit. I really wanted to work with Ryan Sanders, who was the CEO, and with the team. I came in as the operations manager in the middle of COVID.

Three weeks later, the General Manager left, and I became GM. Five days after that, we went into a 110-day lockdown. Because lots of international travelers use our hostels, the lockdown was catastrophic. The minute our country shut its borders, 99 percent of our revenue was gone. Only the guests that were already on site could stay. No new customers. And this went on for 110 days.

We somehow made it through. Then we got an investment from a large company that had a portfolio of legendary properties and were buying more. We went from 5 sites to 15 sites, and from 18 staff members to about 170 today. They represent 51 nationalities at last count. (That is not a typo.) I'm now Chief People Officer.

How did you go from being GM to your new role?

It started at my previous company, where we had to make some really tough decisions and let a lot of people go, including long-term ones. That was horrible. It kind of put me not into a mid-life crisis but a career crisis.

Long story short, I got a coach. She basically made me work my life backward from the end. She made me answer: "When you die, where do you want to be buried? Where do you and your husband want to be in the years right before that? What do you really want to do?", and so on. I worked through that whole thought process.

I realized that I didn't have to change industries but I was more of a people person. I needed to be in a people role more than being a GM allowed me to do. So I sat down with Ryan and politely said that I need to be doing this with or without you guys.

Ryan said: "Well, why don't we have you take on that role here." It wouldn't have happened without having a boss like Ryan. A lot of people would have been like: "OK, see ya."

How would you define the difference between EX and HR as a focus or approach?

I don't come from a traditional HR background, but just in my experience, HR just seems very much focused on the outcome that your business wants, your execs want, your board wants, and less about the people and how you can use people to get that result.

EX is the opposite to me. You're focused on the people because you have to be. Otherwise, the business won't survive. You can use those people's thoughts and ideas to get the business results. That's the main difference for me. I've found a lot of HR professionals are not flexible and don't adapt. "This is the way we're doing it because this is the way we do it."

How did you get interested in employee experience?

It came from Ryan. He knows you (Samantha), and even when I was the GM, he suggested that I join EX Design School. I'd already been reading books about design in general, because I did 3D animation at university. I'm quite interested in design and art. So when I heard there was a design approach to business, I wanted to be a part of it.

Please tell us how you've applied EXD at Haka House.

After the world opened back up and we got that tremendous growth in the number of our properties, it kind of changed who we were. It's been a challenging process to go from a business led by a single entrepreneur to now having investors and stakeholders with various personalities.

We knew we needed to get out there and talk to people, because we'd gone from this 18-person business to a much larger organization with many stakeholders and many approaches and processes.

I decided to do an open discovery, and I started by doing a couple of "Know, Think, Suspect" workshops. (Note: We discuss these workshops in Chapter 8.) One was with leaders to introduce them to EXD, what it means, and why I wanted to go out and do discovery with employees. This first session was all about what they thought we were going to find out in the employee sessions.

After that first session, the operations director said: "I want you to do this with my team," which was the next level down of leaders. So we did another Know, Think, Suspect workshop for those leaders. These workshops gave me solid information, which I could then compare to what employees would tell me about what their experience and struggles were.

What I discovered was really interesting. It turned out that leaders who were the closest to the investors were the ones that were thinking everything was doom and gloom—more than it actually was. I asked everyone: "If you had to rank your employee experience from 1–10, where would it sit?" The leaders came in at around four, and everybody else was about seven.

What did you make of the lower ratings by leaders?

We had something of a cultural difference at first between our parent company and us. The parent company is hugely successful. They own a lot of big, five-star hotels in places like Tahiti. Some of their rooms go for $10,000 a night. They've got a staff person for every possible client need—doormen, concierges, chefs, butlers, and so on.

Meanwhile, the clients for our portfolio are often backpackers, where you have very slim teams because we're not getting the same rates per night. Both hospitality models have worked well, but you can imagine that blending the teams together at the leadership level might come as a shock.

We were sort of sitting back a little bit, sometimes waiting for the parent company to tell us what they wanted. We were almost a little too Kiwi, a little too polite. But they wanted our honest opinions about things. So it's taken until now for us to grow our voice to be like: "No, that won't work." It was kind of a cultural thing, like: "Can we say this?"

The combination of the difference in portfolios, in culture, and different systems meant that leaders were pretty stressed. These workshops helped us to uncover the differences so we could deal with them.

On top of these organizational things, we had the expanding portfolio to consider. They purchased 10 additional properties that were similar to our 5. We needed to rip the guts out of those properties and refurbish them while blending our organizations and systems.

What else came up in those Know, Think, Suspect workshops for leaders?

They were a little scared about me going out to do the discovery. When I asked the leaders: "What do you think the employees will say?", they were all like, "The people are all going to want more money and want to work fewer hours."

The top level of leaders thought that everybody was just going to want more. Then I went to the lower, secondary level of leaders. They said something very different: that employees were going to want more trust, more communication, and want to celebrate more. They made it clear that we haven't really stopped to notice what we've achieved in one year. We need to stop and say, "Look what we've done."

How did the discovery with employees go?

I first invited anyone from the company who wanted to do one. These were one-to-one discussions, from housekeepers to chefs to anyone. What really amazed me about them was that these people were so open with their time. I was a little worried, wondering if these were going to be slugging matches of how terrible we were, but they weren't. I did 22 of these sessions. In some cases, English was not their first language, but it still worked out.

I started with explaining EXD and then asked how they would rate their experience overall. Pretty much they were all relatively high, like seven and eight. But what became glaringly obvious was that communication was an issue. We were relying heavily on our leaders to make sure comms were getting all the way down, and they weren't. Lots of employees didn't have work email addresses, and the messages were just not being delivered in person or any other way. They just didn't know about a lot of things we thought they were being told.

I identified four themes: communication, celebration, trust, and manual processes. By far, communication came up the most.

When I presented to the heads of departments ("HODs") and property managers, they agreed that we had to do something about communication first, and about celebration second. They became two different projects.

Did you have anybody who was just a naysayer? Like, "This is just another fad. I've seen these things come and go. When are we going to be done with this?"

I would say a lot of the HODs were onboard in a verbal way when we were planning. But when it came to taking action on things and going back to them for feedback, it was a struggle. Like, "HR can handle that. We don't really need to be involved."

They weren't against it, but they were also showing that they weren't exactly for it, to the level that they would contribute much to it. If I'm honest, even today there's still a bit of a struggle with some people.

Did anything surprise you after doing the discovery at all levels?

Yes. One of them was that we thought we were going to need all this tech and fancy stuff to communicate to the team, but all they wanted was a newsletter! But let me back up and tell you how we got there.

> *We thought we were going to need all this tech and fancy stuff to communicate to the team, but all they wanted was a newsletter!*

As I said earlier, we identified communication as a big area for improvement. I then wanted to hear from not just employees, but from people in every department; it was important because we have such different teams. If you're a housekeeper, your perspective differs greatly from that of a chef or reservations person. We needed representation from every department to understand what would work.

I sent a basic message saying what we've discovered, what we've been doing, and why we're doing this. Now we need you guys to tell us how to improve communication.

I asked for volunteers and got some from nearly every department. When I didn't get volunteers from a department, I asked the HOD to nominate someone. There were only two of those departments; they did come and actually engage, which was great.

We went through a series of design sessions—what's working and what's not. Then we moved on to the question of okay, where we have communication gaps, what's the best way to fill them?

I had been picturing this complicated solution of creating special Slack channels and other things, plus how that would work with all these different departments. Here's where EXD is so great: I didn't need to have all the answers. None of them wanted anything complicated. They didn't want to download different apps. They simply wanted a newsletter, and they wanted it printed out and put on the notice board!

I was surprised at how passionate people were about solving this issue. Communication is weird because it's something we need, but no one really wants to tackle, given how difficult it can be to find a workable solution.

We have a lot of backpackers working for us. They come on working holiday visas, so this is not their main profession. It turns out that some of these people were graphic designers by training, so they totally got the mission and helped us with communications.

We later compared what the leaders said in the Know, Think, Suspect workshop about communications. They also thought that we'd need some elaborate solution with different apps. The process of designing with, not for, our employees meant we avoided a major rollout that no one wanted after all. It made me feel validated.

Has it been smooth sailing since then?

Not entirely. I still need to have conversations with certain leaders who don't quite get it yet. They don't have a problem with communicating with me. It's not about what I want to say to them. It's about what they want to say to their people and then getting them to take the time and use the newsletter to say it. As with lots of things, it's a work in progress.

What outcomes have you achieved with this project?

Not all of our people have computers, so we send surveys to everyone's devices. We've seen a 50 percent uplift in engagement about things that we've put in these newsletters. We have really varied topics, like how we're doing earthquake strengthening on a lot of buildings; what our Well-Being Team is up to about celebrations; and many other topics.

Here's another focus: Making people aware of the other opportunities we have in the business. We've historically had high turnover. Previously, we might have had a housekeeper who came on a working holiday visa. They might do three months and leave. Since we've been doing the newsletter and letting people know about other opportunities, we now have people who apply and are accepted at other properties. We like that because they're already familiar with our culture and systems, and they seem to enjoy working with us.

We have about 35 employees who are on their fourth and fifth property, and that has only happened since these newsletters started being written. I can't say that it's 100 percent the result of the newsletters, but I can't think of what else would be the cause. Before, we had been giving all the information about openings to leaders, but it clearly was not getting passed along.

> *Discovery has been the single most rewarding thing I've ever done in any of my jobs in my career.*

How did you feel about the discovery process?

Discovery has been the single most rewarding thing I've ever done in any of my jobs in my career. I was really nervous, because before I had ever done it, I worried it was just going to be like: "I want money ... this is a terrible place ... my boss is a jerk...."

But they were so giving of their time, and they just got it. I really didn't expect people at every level to get the point of what we were doing, but they did. It was just humbling and great. It also showed me how much natural passion people had for this business. They wanted to see improvement, but it wasn't from a negative place. It was from the perspective of: "Actually, my employee experience is pretty good."

They were just very open with their thoughts and opinions. A couple of housekeepers I spoke with have become managers at sites. Because of those conversations, I saw some superstars. And we wouldn't have known about them if we weren't having those conversations.

What do you feel are the most important aspects of Employee Experience Design?

If you're going to undertake this, then do what you say you're going to do. Don't just go out and get discovery information and then do nothing with it. I've seen examples of this in other companies I've worked at. We would get lots of employee feedback and then, for one reason or another—whether it's COVID or some other excuse—we did nothing with the information. Another example I've seen is asking employees to co-design events, which they got all excited about. Then someone told them: "Oh sorry, we have no money for those after all." That just kills participation the next time you want feedback.

You don't necessarily have to do all the things they say they want, but you do have to follow up. You have to build that trust, and if you lose it, then it's very hard to get it back.

What are some of the toughest things to convince people of, concerning EXD?

I think it's to give their time. People are just generally super time poor. That means when people are asked to work in a different way, they're naturally resistant to it.

It's interesting that this attitude has not come from the junior staff members, who have been energetic and refreshing. It's more when people higher up see an initiative and their attitude is: *Don't give me anything else to do. I can't handle it.* With Employee Experience Design, I have to keep explaining that actually, if they make time for this, life is going to be a lot easier.

> *With Employee Experience Design, I have to keep explaining that actually, if they make time for this, life is going to be a lot easier.*

Since your communication project, have you had any feedback from leaders who contributed their time?

Definitely. The finance manager, head of revenue, and head of ops were engaged in it 100 percent and they were like, "Oh my God, this is game changing."

My boss, Ryan, has said that he can totally tell the difference in the capability of the leaders who have engaged in EXD and the ones who haven't. The latter group tend to be the ones who mark themselves really high on everything, but the reality is different. They're not communicating with their people. They've not got their finger on the pulse.

In contrast, leaders who have engaged in EXD use elements of it every day, even for small things. So instead of saying: "You're not doing this…," they'll say things like, "How do you think you could get there? And what should I do to enable you to get there?"

And in performance conversations, rather than saying: "You're doing this wrong", they ask: "What do you think is going wrong here?", or "How do you think we can get to where we need to be?" It's engaging for ideas instead of just telling.

There are a few leaders who've been around a long time and are very much like: "I'm the one that knows. You don't know." Their teams tend to struggle.

How would you describe how the parent company has reacted to EXD?

The CEO went on a tour recently of every one of our properties. It was just him and one other person because Ryan couldn't go, so it's not like we could spin some EXD narrative about what he was seeing.

He talked to a lot of team members and asked questions about what's working and what's not. The last time he went around, they were like, "Everything's fine." This time, he said they were confident to say what they thought, like: "[This thing] is not working. You're spending money on it and it doesn't work."

He asked me why they were so confident to speak up this time. I said we have a Communication Playbook and in it we talk about ways they can tell us what's working and what is not. We were inviting the direct feedback. He thought it was an amazing change.

If you found an organization that could really use some help, what would be the first actions that you might recommend that they do?

It would be to go out and get to know your people. Spend some time with them. Even take a shift doing one of their jobs. I found the benefit of getting direct experience on the operational side of things the hard way during COVID. We had a period where we didn't have any staff at all for one property. All the usual staff had COVID, and we had a fully booked property for a group. I had to go up there and run the property: I mean doing housekeeping, check-ins, everything by myself. If I didn't have that experience, I couldn't talk to the people with as much conviction as I have now. Otherwise, people will just look at a leader and think *You don't know what you're talking about.*

Knowing what you know about EXD and thinking about the organizations you've been part of, what would you do differently if you had a second chance?

Probably speak up more. I don't really mean in my current company, because that's happening. But if I could do things differently, I would have been who I am, which is a person who speaks up more.

I don't know if it's a woman thing, a Kiwi thing, or both. Sometimes we can be: "No worries, you guys just do it your way." But I think it doesn't serve the people you're leading and the people in your business if you don't speak up about something you notice and feel strongly about.

Why do you suppose more organizations don't apply and benefit from taking an EX design approach?

I think people sometimes think it's a bit fluffy and they don't really understand the impact of it. They also think it's going to cost both time and money.

And if they ask employees what would improve their experience, they'll just want to work less and be paid more. They're frightened.

What was the structure of the discovery one-on-ones? Did you invite them to chat over coffee, or was it in a conference room or over Zoom?

We're geographically spread across New Zealand. If the budget had allowed, I would have loved to go to every site, but I only had in-person conversations with those in Auckland. For everyone else, it was a video call at a time of their choosing, because a lot of them have pretty rigid schedules. They also had to find a private space to talk, and some of our staff live in dorm rooms with other people.

Did you give them questions ahead of time to think about, or were you just asking questions on the spot?

Ahead of time, I gave them an overview of why I was talking with people and what I hoped the outcome would be, in terms of their honest opinions.

When we met, I started it with an overview of what EXD was, and what I wanted them to tell me; in other words, their true feelings. Some of them just kind of launched in. For others, I had to ask a few questions before they were comfortable to chat.

How many of those people seemed nervous at the beginning and they might have been thinking: *I'm talking to this person—could my job be at stake?*

I'd say probably 80 percent were like, *What does she want with me?* But remember, I had asked for volunteers. Even so, they were probably curious and a bit scared, like, *How's this going to end?*

Usually, the first 15 minutes were a bit light. You could tell they were holding back. But I made sure to tell them that what they were sharing with me would not go anywhere in terms of identifying them individually. I would not share that with anyone. The only thing that I would share with others was themes, and I'd share those themes with them before I shared them with anybody else.

This was interesting for the leaders because some of them said: "I want the full conversations." I told them: "You're not getting them. You just have to trust, because otherwise I will not get honesty."

Did word get around after a while that: "It's OK to talk with Kirsty?"

I thought I had finished my discovery, but I started to hear that someone else wants to talk with me, and then other people as well. Keep in mind that we're geographically spread across New Zealand, and some of our properties are way up in the mountains where we don't make many site visits.

But from that discovery, word has spread and the HR team and I will often get direct emails from people when they're not happy or there's some issue going on. We didn't get those emails before.

I want them to know that they're not isolated on that site. There is someone they can call who is going to listen. And I've never even met many of these people.

Do you think you're getting that kind of information earlier than you would have before, and before it grows into a larger problem?

Yes, I am. It's really interesting when we have leadership meetings and I'll bring up a topic. Someone will say: "How do you know that?" I'll say: "Because somebody in the housekeeping team told me." They're like, "Oh."

We can get on top of things. Sometimes these aren't performance matters, but some other issue going on. When we dig a little, we find out that there's a whole lot of things going on interpersonally that we didn't know about. We're careful with that information, but it really helps us do our job for the business.

What are some things you've learned from mentors over the years?

I've worked with a lot of amazing leaders. I've been lucky. But one that really stood out to me was Tom Ruddenklau. He was leading at Jucy when we went into COVID. If you looked at Tom "on paper" he doesn't look like a glitzy leader. But he did two things that have stayed with me for years.

First, he was caring, but firm. We went through all the pandemic stuff and then got sold into receivership. He literally sat us all down and was like, "You're either on the bus or you're off the bus. Yes, we've been sold, but we need to move on." His honesty was a great employee experience for me, rather than beating around the bush.

The other thing he used to do was he personally wrote Christmas cards to everyone. I know it sounds absolutely ridiculous, but literally everyone in the business got one, and it was personally written. It wasn't just "Merry Christmas," but he'd be like, "I really was impressed with this thing you did this year." I was like, *really?* He was a very humble leader. You'd do anything for him because of those small things. He taught me that those really tiny things and making time for people is super important.

Sometimes I struggle, because I definitely do make time for a lot of people, and sometimes that's really hard on my workload. Occasionally, I have to hide so I can get some stuff done! But I know how much it meant to me, so I try to be available.

Another thing I learned and I always say to my team is *you never cancel your one-on-one with anyone on your team.* If they want to cancel it because they don't have anything to talk about, that's fine. You never cancel it.

> You never cancel your one-on-one with anyone on your team.

Thank you so much, Kirsty. It was great to hear how you've implemented EX Design in your interesting organization in New Zealand!

You're very welcome.

Chapter Summary

Kirsty defines Employee Experience as being focused on people to achieve business results, contrasting it with traditional HR's outcome-first approach.

Through direct discovery with employees (one-on-one discussions), Kirsty found that the primary employee pain points were lack of communication, desire for more celebration, trust, and issues with manual processes, rather than just more money or fewer hours.

The team implemented a simple, employee-designed solution for communication: a printed newsletter, demonstrating that effective solutions don't always require complex technology.

EXD outcomes included a 50 percent uplift in engagement related to newsletter topics and an increase in internal mobility and retention among employees moving to different properties.

Kirsty emphasizes the critical importance of doing what you say you're going to do, with feedback to build and maintain employee trust in the EXD process.

PART III
Design

7

Culture Check

Moments That Matter and Moments of Truth

Any discussion of organizational change needs to include at least one fundamental question: *What's the FROM and TO? We want to change from what to what?*

The "from what" part of that question is what we want to discuss in this chapter. Of course, you can assess an organization's current condition on many dimensions: What is the attrition rate; what is our conversion rate from offer to acceptance; what learning and development challenges do we have; and so on.

What we want to focus on are some aspects of the culture. We have two fundamental concepts you need to know. They will become part of your regular vocabulary when discussing your organization as it relates to EXP.

Moments That Matter

What is your organizational culture in the first place? One major aspect of that culture is what we discussed in Chapter 5—the Employee Value Proposition. As you will recall, that is the combination of pay, benefits, work environment, career and learning opportunities, policies, and other elements that an organization offers in exchange for employees working there.

We also mentioned in Chapter 2 that it's common for people to say: "We already focus on employee experience" when what they mean is they have a few things in place like a survey, or employee onboarding.

> *"Moments that Matter."* That term refers to moments you design and execute, or that have spontaneously happened and then have become traditions.

We have a term for certain aspects of a culture—they are "Moments that Matter." That term refers to moments you design and execute, or that have spontaneously happened and then have become traditions.

Maybe one of the oldest corporate Moments that Matter is when employees traditionally would receive a gold watch upon reaching some anniversary with the company. Airbnb replaced that tradition with one of its own and instead it set up and funded a social impact account. Employees could choose their nonprofit and on those anniversaries, the fund made a donation in the employee's name to that organization.

Other Moments that Matter are when organizations may carefully design the first day for employees, when they arrange special meetings with senior people, assign a "buddy" to help them get acclimated, and so on. One moment at a place we worked had a ship's bell that someone rang when the department met certain goals.

Moments that Matter might merely be borrowed from other organizations (like the gold watch tradition) or they can be unique to the organization and really give you a flavor of the culture. Two examples of unique Moments that Matter happened at Patagonia.

You need to know about Chipper Bro, because he was the first person I met at Patagonia. I walked in and there was a giant wood desk in the reception area. Behind it was a dude with curly hair and bare feet. He alternated between flipping a Frisbee and working a yoyo. He's like: "Hey how you doin today! Get over here and sit down! It's so good to see you! I'm Chipper Bro."

I'm like: "Excuse me? I didn't catch your name?"

"It's Chipper Bro." (He changed his name to that.)

"Well nice to meet you ... Mr. Bro."

Fast forward—because I was head of HR, Chipper ended up being on my team. It was not unusual for him to be missing from work for several hours.

My assumption was that he had been at the beach, given that he often returned with wet hair and sandy feet.

Anyway, Chipper was loved by me and pretty much everyone, and he was central to an important Moment that Matters at Patagonia: He ran the surf camp. Every year Chipper would pad down to the highway and put a sign over the giant Ventura, California exit sign on the highway that read:

> CHIPPER'S SURF CAMP
>
> ALOHA FESTIVAL

Completely illegal. All the new Patagonia people would head to the beach, and Chipper would have boards and wetsuits ready for us.

Chipper's whiteboard was the sand. He'd explain: "This is the tide … these are the waves. This is you surfing, this is you falling down, this is me helping you back up…" all with helpful stick figures written in the sand.

One of the new hires wasn't surfing. I was like: "Hey why aren't you surfing?" She goes: "I don't swim. I don't want to mess up my hair." She felt excluded because swimming wasn't her thing. I later adjusted this tradition so if you wanted to surf, cool. If you're not into surfing, you could do rock climbing or visit a farm that's also accessible by wheelchair.

My onboarding surf day was one of the favorite days of my life. It was that way for most people there: We're at the ocean and see the mountains way off in the distance. It's during working hours, and we're barefoot in the sand on the beach with Chipper.

I could go on and on about the Moments that Matter at Patagonia. One time a guy slammed my laptop closed and goes: "Surf's up. Let's go." Another time, a woman looked at me: "Do you have flip flops?" I go: "Um, yeah I own some, but I usually wear these tennis shoes." She looked at me: "Uh uh. Not here. Either you don't wear shoes, or you wear flip flops."

People worked hard at Patagonia, so don't get the wrong idea. But the signs of the culture were everywhere, just like all the beach towels draped around the Patagonia campus, drying in the sun. Oh, and the guy in a completely worn and tattered leather apron, wailing away with a sledgehammer in an old tin shed in the center of the campus? That's Yvon Chouinard, the founder.

I'll just mention one other Moment: The Paddle Out. There was a guy, Micah, who had been with Patagonia basically forever. He was beloved by a lot of people but was rough around the edges. The only place I could put him where he could do good work and not get into too much trouble was working in the Patagonia Archives. It was a repository for the history of Patagonia, including all the clothing we made over the years, all the causes we supported, and so on. I spent a lot of time in the archives and with Micah, because I wanted to understand Patagonia's culture and history as deeply as I could.

Back to the Paddle Out: A while after I had left Patagonia, Micah passed away way too young, after years of struggling with cancer. The tradition when an event like that happens is we all meet on the beach, paddle out, and say goodbye to our friend. Keep in mind that this was after I had left the company and after Yvon had transferred ownership to a trust and a nonprofit. Yvon was on a large yellow surfboard in the water next to me and said: "Hey thanks for coming."

Talk about Moments that Matter: We're both no longer officially connected to the company; we're there for a guy who is no longer on this Earth. This tradition was not the result of some focus group, nor was it part of a press release to build the brand. It was simply what you did if you had the spirit of Patagonia.

Think about your organization. What are things that people do even if they're not required to do them? Then think about the best places you've worked and the rituals you remember. Sometimes the most meaningful ritual can happen when someone makes a spontaneous suggestion; or it's just the thing you do when you're a surfer in California.

If you're not the "Culture Keeper," then seek out that person who knows the history, culture, and traditions. If you care about the organization and the culture that drives it, then it's worth preserving.

I made a real effort to become as knowledgeable as I could about the traditions and history of Patagonia. I spent a great many hours in the archives. My hope one day was to perhaps be a philosopher or wear overalls in a trailer on the edge of campus and tell stories—my own small effort to help keep a very precious culture living for future generations to take up.

I've been in a LOT of organizations that had thriving cultures that died because the stories and traditions were replaced by spreadsheets and annual reports. If you're not the "Culture Keeper," then seek out that person who knows the history, culture, and traditions. If you care about the organization and the culture that drives it, then it's worth preserving. Certainly, you can't force people to observe traditions, but some people seek and keep them because they "get it." These moments can become some of the best memories and learning moments people have, when looking back on their entire work career.

Moments of Truth

The operative word here is "truth." Moments of Truth are what *really happens* in an organization. Keep two things in mind: First, they are frequently but not always negatives or shortcomings, as you'll see in a moment. And second, Moments of Truth will sometimes completely match the expectation or even exceed it.

> *Moments of Truth are* what *really happens* in *an organization.*

Moments of Truth are like a high-resolution video feed of an organization. They are not what the organization says about itself, but what it does. They're actions that send a message, even if the message sender sometimes was unaware that anything was being sent, and the result was unintentional. Here are nine examples of Moments of Truth:

1. We mentioned in Chapter 3 about how the recruiting coordinators were not recognized along with other people for their efforts in bringing on new hires. Unintentional message: Other units are more important.
2. What we hear every day as consumers when we call companies: "Your call is very important to us." Moment of Truth: You're kept on hold, then an AI bot attempts to answer your question because we don't staff the unit with humans. Subtext: Your call is not *that* important to us.
3. An employee announces that she is pregnant. How the manager reacts and then responds can be a massive Moment of Truth about how supportive the organization is to women.

4. At Town Hall meetings or other big events like annual or quarterly meetings, what topics get talked about first? Is it employee safety? Is it customer satisfaction? Or is it financial results, sales goals, and new products and services? They might all be important, but the order sends a message.
5. What is the meeting culture in terms of how close to on time they begin? Is the time set by a senior person but the meeting only starts when that person shows up? Is the senior person on time, occasionally late, or always late? If it's a chronic pattern, then the message is: *My time is more important than all of your time put together.*
6. It's common for uniforms to be worn in retail and service organizations. Who chooses what they look like?
7. On a more micro level, think back to planning meetings you've been in. It's common for someone to be the "scribe"—very often a woman—who captures ideas on a flip chart. Have you noticed any occasions when all the thoughts from senior people get recorded but the contributions of more junior people—again this is frequently true for women—don't tend to get recorded quite as often?
8. Who gets input on what the organization's new logo will be? True story: A large insurance company spent a lot of money and time on a rebranding effort. After many months, it came down to two final versions: one was gold and crimson, and one was gold and blue. The chairman wanted to make the right decision, so he waited until the annual meeting of all the office managers from around the country. The climax of the annual event was going to be a vote by the managers: "So you each have two business cards—one for each color. When you file out of this hall, just put the card you prefer in the goldfish bowls our people are holding near the door. May the best design win." The office managers chose the crimson-and-gold one. The chairman wanted the blue-and-gold version. So the blue-and-gold version it is!
9. Here's another insight into the Patagonia culture, specifically relating to childcare. After I (Dean) was hired as the head of HR, I inherited a few projects in different stages of completion. One of them was a childcare center in our Reno, Nevada warehouse that was in the works, but its opening would be delayed two or three months due to construction issues. As one of my first tasks, I thought I'd write a note

to the leadership team and founders with an update. It ended with: "I just wanted to make sure you knew the status, OK?"

Yvon's wife, a pioneer who co-founded on-site childcare at Patagonia decades ago, shot back in all caps. It went something like this:

> Dean, it is not "OK." Here's what you're going to do immediately, as in today: you will let every single woman who is breastfeeding go home on paid leave, effective immediately. We will not have a single day that a mom cannot breastfeed her child in this company. So as of right now, they're all on paid leave. They can go home and take care of their children until this thing is built. Tell them we're so sorry it's late."

Talk about actions that support promises. There was no doubt about how I would support nursing parents going forward. I could go on with other examples, like how campus space for childcare was a higher priority over space for the adults working there.

As a side note from Dean: Some years before Patagonia, I had been CHRO for Fossil Group, which had 8,000 employees in 23 countries. There I had chosen not to implement on-site childcare due to cost and insurance issues. I remember my own experience of taking my young daughter to a separate childcare center every day, and how I missed countless moments and connections that I could have had if she had been a short walk away from my office. When I multiply my loss by the many thousands of people who worked at Fossil and also had families, this decision is the greatest regret of my entire career.

> *When I multiply my loss by the many thousands of people who worked at Fossil and also had families, this decision is the greatest regret of my entire career.*

Moments of Truth Are Often Spontaneous

We once had an Airbnb event in Paris, attended by 7,000 hosts and 650 employees. In the midst of this event, Paris was the target of some terrorist attacks. Once we found that no attendees were injured or killed, the focus became getting everyone home safely and to manage the mental health of those that were affected by this tragedy. When the flights finally landed back in San Francisco, around 50 employees met us at the airport with baked goods, Welcome Back signs, and lots of hugs. This was a self-organized reaction when those who didn't get to make the trip to Paris heard about the challenges we faced and decided to ensure we were welcomed back. It was a great example of how the mission came to life, the culture was democratized, and a sense of belonging was strong within the Airbnb "family."

Chapter Summary

Moments that Matter are designed or spontaneously adopted traditions that shape culture, like the traditional gold watch for long service (replaced by Airbnb's social impact accounts), Patagonia's surf camp, or the "Paddle Out" ritual.

Moments of Truth reveal what really happens in an organization, often exposing shortcomings or unintentional messages through actions rather than stated values (for example, unrecognized recruiting coordinators, long customer service hold times, delayed childcare at Patagonia, and a manager's reaction to pregnancy).

These moments are crucial because they send powerful messages about what the organization truly values, even if those messages are unintended or painful.

Although Moments that Matter are often pre-planned, Moments of Truth can occur at any magnitude and any time, offering a "high-resolution video feed" of the culture.

8

Three Frameworks

A Structure for Achieving Meaningful Design

We've discussed how Employee Experience Design is not a thing you plug in and turn on, but mainly a mindset, ways of working, and a different way of organizing what was the HR function. We also just talked about how to get a handle on some aspects of your culture by understanding both Moments that Matter and Moments of Truth.

Now it's time to talk about some ways you can begin to improve that culture. By the end of this chapter, you will have a strong handle on the many important processes and tools at your disposal as you co-design elements of your employee experience.

The Importance of Design

In Chapter 1, we talked about how "Employee Experience" has been around since 2013, when it was born at Airbnb, and how EXD is significantly different. That one word of "Design" makes such a difference. It's why we as consumers love how some products delight us in how they work so intuitively and effectively.

The Design Brief

When designers are asked to take on a new project, the first thing they do is look for—or create—a design brief. This is a mandatory starting point of any design challenge. It is critical to the success of designing something new, because it lays out the boundaries that the team needs to work within.

It may be tempting to think that "action takers" don't waste time on creating documents, and how they should "get going with the real work" instead. That would be a mistake that could turn into a disaster: It's this kind of ready-fire-aim approach that leads to scope creep, cost overruns, and friction within teams.

On one level, the design brief simply answers the question: "What are we trying to achieve with this project?" But there is a structure to the brief that makes it even more explicit and useful for achieving the goals of the project.

Here are the *traditional* elements of a design brief:

- Project scope
- Goals
- Audience
- Budget
- Timeline
- Deliverables
- Other known constraints

We recommend that you include as many of those elements as you can, but that you **not get bogged down by them**. If you're embarking on a major initiative, then all these elements need to be thought out.

Think of it this way: If you don't do a design brief and just launch into a project, these elements will happen anyway: There will be some scope that may or may not grow; either a budget will be allocated or not; there will be some expectation of a delivery date, though people may disagree on it; and so on. It makes so much more sense to address these elements ahead of time to the best of the team's ability. Perhaps no one yet knows the budget—fine, then you can say: "Budget: TBD (To Be Determined)."

Let's say you want to apply EXD when you create a relatively quick policy about bringing pets into the office. In that case, it might make sense to have an abbreviated version.

Here's what we think is the minimum you need for any design brief to be effective:

1. **Start with the phrase: "How might we ...."** This is crucial because it solicits multiple approaches to the outcome by asking "How." Then the word "might" also allows for brainstorming. Notice how saying: "How might we ..." comes across entirely differently from: "Find the solution to ..."
2. **Include the phrase: "... so that ..."** This emphasizes the "why" behind the project and enables everyone to agree with the goals. It also sets the stage if people disagree and want to state what they think the outcome should be. We either have consensus or know what to discuss in order to reach consensus.

It's always important to tie the "so that ..." to one or more organizational outcomes, as we discussed in Chapter 3.

Here are two examples of the minimum design brief:

"How might we create a clear and inclusive pet policy so that employees can bring pets to work without disrupting others' comfort, safety, and productivity?"

"How might we design a leadership program so that it not only helps people to grow and develop, but will also help them to take ownership and feel valued?"

As with pretty much all aspects of EXD, this document can change, and is likely to. After people roll up their sleeves and wade into a project, constraints and opportunities become evident that weren't clear at the beginning.

Let's say we started work on the pets-to-office policy, and someone contacted the building's owner about the lease, which said nothing about pets. We might uncover some constraints, or even some new opportunities: Maybe a tenant on another floor already has an effective space for pets and humans to coexist, so the timeline might get adjusted.

The PREP Framework

We hope we've effectively made the point that Employee Experience Design has great potential to change many aspects of your organization for the better. Sometimes that realization can make people wonder where to begin. After all, if you think at a granular level about all the experiences you have in the course of one day, it can be overwhelming. And that's just one employee for one day.

PREP breaks down the broad concept of employee experience into four key types of experiences that employees have at work: Purpose, Relationships, Enablement, and Performance.

This is where the PREP Framework can help. We already gave advice in Chapter 5 on Mindsets that it's important to start small—but just to get started. A great way to do that is to start with this framework.

PREP breaks down the broad concept of employee experience into four key types of experiences that employees have at work: Purpose, Relationships, Enablement, and Performance. Let's look at each one.

1. Purpose Experiences in the PREP Framework

These experiences are related to an employee's sense of meaning and purpose at work. Many organizations can point to having a "Mission Statement"; sometimes these documents may be worse than worthless: It's not uncommon for a task force to take many months and dozens of drafts to come up with the statement—that says nothing and gets filed away. Does the following sound like something you might have seen somewhere?

"Our mission is to leverage innovative synergies and scalable solutions to empower stakeholders, drive value-added outcomes, and optimize holistic paradigms for sustainable growth in a dynamic global ecosystem."

Contrast that with Airbnb's simple statement, which was: "Anyone can belong anywhere." There, the concept of belonging and connections became huge. In fact, we did some deep research into people's attitudes when staying at Airbnb properties. It turns out that the core of the offering was not the physical space that was being rented. It was the connection that the host facilitated and the overall experience; it's like the difference between renting a house and renting a home. We worked to tie our employees to that mission through the $1,000 annual vouchers to stay in Airbnb properties.

In Chapter 7, we talked about how Moments of Truth give you insights into whether organizations are walking the talk, as they say. Think about the following key questions as they apply to your organization:

Key Question: How do we know whether employees understand the mission and how their work directly supports it? Some organizations have pretty obvious missions, like a nonprofit that provides health clinics in low-income neighborhoods. However, it may be that managers have never made an explicit effort to tie their team's efforts to the overall goal—and recognize each individual for those efforts.

Let's say the clinic headquarters has a Comms team whose job it is to create marketing materials for the clinics, manage paid advertising at bus stops, create signage, and so on. It's easy for KPIs (Key Performance Indicators) to be created along the lines of: "Increase the click-through rates of our Google Ads to 5 percent or higher by Q4." Though that may be an important KPI for the clinics, it's sterile: Where is the connection to the mission?

Right away a possible EXD project comes to mind, in the form of a design brief:

"How might we review and revise KPIs across the organization, so that all employees can see in writing how their KPIs are connected to the clinic's mission to support our neighborhoods?"

This is a perfect example of how an EXD effort can cost nothing to implement (except a little time), and can have a potentially significant effect on employee morale and retention. It reminds us of the fable of a person who walked by a construction site where brick masons were working. She asked the first mason she saw: "What are you doing?" The mason said: "What does it look like I'm doing? I'm laying bricks." She walked on and asked the next mason the same question. He said: "I'm building a wall." She continued up to the third mason and asked the same question. He said: "I'm building a cathedral." All three of them were correct, but maybe only one of them was inspired.

Key Question: How do we foster a culture where the organization's values are evident in daily actions and ethical behavior? If you have a culture that loves being outdoors, then you let them surf when the surf is up. Then, to minimize your impact on the planet, everyone is served the same food, usually vegan to decrease waste and lessen the effect on the planet. Of course, you would have no single-use plastic serving items on campus. If you have a culture that loves video games, maybe you provide free Red Bull and comfy couches to play games during breaks.

Culture isn't a class or a program; it needs to show up every day in every way in your choices of what you do—and don't do. For example, employees at the Patagonia Reno warehouse wanted more access to organic food grown locally. So, Patagonia dug up a parking lot and installed a full, employee-run organic, regenerative garden that supplied food for the warehouse every day.

Key Question: How do we create opportunities for employees to see the impact of their work and celebrate successes that align with the organization's mission? This is so important because as we said in Chapter 1, EXD is not a once-and-done proposition. Some people have likened it to being one of those performers on stage, where they get lots of plates spinning on sticks. It's spellbinding because the performer has to spin up the plates continuously or they'll crash. Other people look at EXD like planting a garden: You need patience to see results at first, but then you're more than paid back. Even the best gardens need regular tending to get rid of pests and so forth.

At Patagonia, all employees could apply for a multi-week paid environmental internship anywhere in the world. When they returned from their adventure, we were invited to sit on the floor in the Grand Room and listen while they showed videos and photos and told inspiring stories about the impact they made.

About a very different kind of impact someone made at Patagonia: One day we received a call from a national magazine asking Patagonia's head of Marketing: "Have you seen what's in your shorts?" What we didn't know was that an employee in the design department—without permission—had the words "Vote The Assholes Out" (meaning people who didn't support climate action) sewn into the back of the tag on the shorts. His idea was celebrated and shared on campus. We sold more of those shorts than ever before and spent zero on that "marketing campaign."

Earlier I (Mark) mentioned that I had an awful job after law school, where it felt like we were trying to catch people doing something wrong. If organizations want to cultivate a great employee experience, they need to catch people doing things right.

We discussed in Chapter 3 how Airbnb had a job interview process first for the skills necessary in a position and then for compatibility between the mission and values of the company and those of job candidates. Employees were central to this interviewing process relating to mission and values, and they could see the direct connection between their candidate evaluations and who got hired—or not.

Another area where the company and employees could point to a lot of successes was our company-wide volunteer efforts. First, Airbnb provided employees with four hours of paid volunteer time each month. A key aspect of the program was we helped employees to engage with causes they cared about. We also had volunteering at a local food bank as part of the onboarding process. It was a great way for the company to connect with the community, but it also made it easy for new hires to get to know each other in this shared experience. It also demonstrated the company's commitment to social impact.

These individual and group volunteer activities not only fostered a sense of purpose beyond their daily tasks, but our research showed that around 90 percent of employees felt that the opportunities allowed them to connect with other co-workers in ways beyond what their "regular job" provided.

Another way we tried to showcase employees' skills and passions was through the "First Thursdays" program. On that day of each month, any employee could sign up to lead a course or workshop on a topic of interest to them. Some of the topics were just that—interesting to that person but not related to work—like bicycle maintenance and margarita making. Other topics had more obvious connections to work, like coding for beginners and angel investing.

If we come back to the idea of design briefs, we could write one as follows:

"How might we use the company's existing systems so that more employees could see the effect they and their colleagues have on the company's mission?"

There are so many benefits to designing with employees instead of for them. It might be that some IT folks know of capabilities that people in HR would not: For instance, someone might have the idea of training a recently developed AI agent on an internal database of weekly reports and meeting notes from across the company. In that case, AI would do the heavy lifting to tie employee activities to the mission.

Another employee might have a decidedly low-tech approach to the same challenge: Try out a color-coding system that matches KPIs at the employee level to company outcomes. With the mindset of starting small, a few people could quickly do some testing and determine if this idea had merit.

We can recommend an excellent book to you called *The Max Strategy*.[1] It's a quick read about two people who get stranded at an airport and one of them has many lessons from a long life in business. Anyway, one of the points that's stuck with us is the concept that: "Experiments never fail." What the person, Max, means is that you can always learn something from an experiment, even if it seemed to not deliver the results you were after. It can be liberating to adopt the mindset of quickly trying some things out early on and getting insights that were not visible before you ran the quick test.

We just went over a number of "Purpose" experiences, or the first "P" in the PREP model. Now let's look at the next element.

2. Relationship Experiences in the PREP Framework

Relationship experiences pertain to all the interactions and connections that employees have at work, whether with their colleagues, managers, or others across the organization.

This is such a large segment of life at work for just about everyone. Sure, there may be a handful of "lone wolves" or individual contributors who are highly specialized and have limited interactions with others. But for the most part, employees get things done by working with others on just about everything.

People who study organizational dynamics will tell you that there are many phases that people must go through before they become a highly effective group. Most of that discussion is beyond the scope of this handbook, but let's look at some main areas where we could potentially focus an Employee Experience Design effort.

Key Question: How do we create opportunities for team building and connections among colleagues?

We've all been there: A new team is formed, and things are awkward on several levels. First, some people know each other very well—or perhaps

---

[1] Dauten, Dale. *The Max Strategy: How to Make Your Business a Big Success.* New York: William Morrow, 1997.

too well. The people who know each other and get along will sit together and also exchange knowing glances during discussions. Those who know each other "too well" might be rivals, incompatible personalities, or downright enemies. It's in this context that new people are brought into the mix.

Let's say you are a manager who's been around the block a few times. You were told to assemble a group and didn't have the luxury of creating your Dream Team. You have a bunch of people with a bunch of interpersonal dynamics going on—but you have a task to get done. What do you do?

This is where you could use some help from people across the organization to create the conditions for team success. The very first team activity could be the following design brief:

"How might we fast-track trust and connection in our new team, so we can work well together and achieve our goals?"

That's kind of the Holy Grail, right? If only we knew how to do this earlier in our careers. And talk about tying activities to business outcomes: The organization has lots of teams going at any one time, so improving team dynamics and effectiveness can pay huge dividends.

> *"How might we fast-track trust and connection in our new team, so we can work well together and achieve our goals?"*

Your next step could be to recruit a handful of experienced people for some efficiently run meetings to address the design brief. (Soon we will give you specific tools for conducting those EXD meetings effectively.)

Let's say you made progress on creating that cohesive team. The next challenge when it comes to "Relationship Experiences" is how the team will get down to business. It's important to note that truly effective teams are not "Mr. Rogers' Neighborhoods" where we all smile, get along, and have fun. People are often busy and stressed even before coming to a meeting. They bring their questions, opinions, and objections to the project and are not sure when they should be honest, if ever.

The meeting leader has the opportunity to create an excellent team environment, even if the entire organization is not run quite as well. People get attuned quickly to how things typically work in organizations, based upon their painful experience there and at other places they worked. It often boils down to *keep your head down, do your job, don't make waves,* and so on. It's against this "lived experience" that the leader needs to explain how we'll be doing things differently. How everyone needs to be respectful but at the same time, honest. That means if you disagree, you need to say so, while focusing on the topic under discussion and not on the person discussing it.

Some team members may still be hesitant to say what they really think, because it can be scary to do so. This is where the skill of the meeting leader comes in. Depending on the makeup of the group, maybe the meeting minutes should not be written down, so people feel like their opinions won't come back to haunt them. Or maybe the meeting leader needs to model the desired behavior. However it's done, the goal is worth working toward—a small group of people who are honest, assertive but not aggressive, and respectful of others.

On this topic of creating connections between colleagues, there's a common myth that when people work from home, they become increasingly depressed and less collaborative. At Guild, we were a "remote first" culture and knew about the challenges of working from home. We therefore asked a team of employees to address those challenges.

After exploring several ideas, they recommended creating a new fractional role called "Community Captains." They analyzed where people lived within a two-hour drive radius and designated a captain for each territory of that size. Employees not only designed the role but then could apply for it. They were paid more to take this on, in addition to their existing responsibilities.

The pre-post survey indicated that fully remote employees that were actively engaged by a Community Captain were more energized and collaborative than employees coming to work in the office every day. This is EXD at its finest: A group of employees creates and designs a role to solve an EX problem—one that everyone *still* assumes is unsolvable.

Fully remote employees that were actively engaged by a Community Captain were more energized and collaborative than employees coming to work in the office every day.

When the going gets rough

Few organizations have effective systems for heated disagreements to take place without unfortunate consequences. In her excellent book, *Radical Candor*,[2] Kim Scott talked about how she saw just such a system at work at Google.

---

[2] Scott, Kim. *Radical Candor: How to Get What You Want by Saying What You Mean.* London, UK: Pan Books, 2019.

Three Frameworks

A guy named Matt Cutts was a senior engineer at Google. Even so, he was a few layers removed from Larry Page, the co-founder. Kim was new to Google when she found herself in a meeting with Matt and Larry to discuss a proposal. The two had different opinions, and Matt couldn't get Larry to come around. Things went south from there, with Matt literally yelling at Larry, and saying that his approach would flood Matt's unit with "so much crap" that they'd never be able to keep up.

Kim was highly experienced, but Google's culture was new to her. She wondered whether she was witnessing a career-limiting move by Matt, and she glanced over at Larry. He was smiling and apparently enjoying the debate. This made a real impression on Kim about how—at least with Larry—you were expected to speak your mind in no uncertain terms.

Even if someone is not a founder, it's necessary to invite and reinforce the kind of honesty you're looking to receive. We think you may agree that it's rare to find groups where complete honesty about ideas is encouraged; but when you do find yourself in such a group, it can be one of the best team experiences of your career.

> *It's necessary to invite and reinforce the kind of honesty you're looking to receive.*

3. Enabling Experiences in the PREP Framework

Enabling experiences are ones that focus on providing employees with the tools, resources, processes, and work environment necessary for them to do their jobs effectively.

I (Samantha) brought up in Chapter 5 how each day we have consumer-grade expectations during our life outside of work. When we then arrive at work, it can feel like we've gone through a time warp to an era before accessible information, immediate availability of products, and so on.

Because all of us are thoroughly acquainted with the remarkable services and tools we have as consumers these days, this portion of the PREP Framework really lends itself to a large number of EXD efforts.

We know someone who got a PhD from Cambridge University in England and was a rocket scientist. He liked to describe his efforts when improving a system as "progressive de-bottlenecking." Other people will refer to it as "finding the limiting factor." Either way, almost all organizations would benefit from an effort along the lines of this design brief:

> "How can we objectively determine what systems and technologies our employees have the most difficulty using, so that solving those challenges will improve their job satisfaction and increase their productivity?"

The solution is more complicated than simply doing a survey. The survey approach may be one option, but another could be to interview users or even sit with them as they go about their daily tasks.

This is where the mindset of "Find the why" comes in. A small team could develop an interview/observation process that's designed to focus on a single employee at a time. The interviewer could have the survey the employee filled out as a starting point. Then the discussion turns to the main tools this person uses to do their job.

The goal of this session is to do two things: First, to have the employee explain the pain points they have throughout the day with systems:

- "I get logged out of this app continuously throughout the day for no apparent reason. Then I need to apologize to customers on the phone and ask them to repeat the information. We're both frustrated."
- "The way the information is displayed over here does not match how this other system wants to see it, so I need to be jotting down notes all day long, and that leads to input errors."
- "I get a migraine from looking at certain monitors we have around the office, but sometimes those are the only ones available."

Second, the interviewer/observer could get other clues and insights just by watching how the employee uses the systems:

> "I noticed that you close one window and open another repeatedly. Is that because you prefer it, or did anyone show you the way to jump between them with a simple key combination?"
>
> "You were showing me how you need to look in an online folder to assemble all the flyers and fact sheets for when the team goes on the

road to trade shows. Do people sometimes bring outdated fact sheets because they get confused, given that it looks like there is no naming convention for files?"

This kind of deep dive can pay dividends: Solving problems with technology and tools rarely benefits just one person. Also, this is a perfect example of the EXD mindset of "iterate": We can look to fix some low-hanging fruit issues and then come back later for more challenging problems.

> This is a perfect example of the EXD mindset of "iterate": We can look to fix some low-hanging fruit issues and then come back later for more challenging problems.

The bad news with systems is they continuously change. The good news: There are continual opportunities to see if people are aware of new features that can save them time and grief.

The "Enabling" piece of the PREP Framework covers a lot more than technology. It also covers:

- Designing efficient processes.
- Creating safe, comfortable, and well-equipped physical workspaces.
- Offering effective training and development opportunities.
- Creating effective onboarding and offboarding experiences.
- (We all had a crash course about the following during COVID): Ensuring that employees can participate in meetings from anywhere and have access to the systems and information they need.

When I (Mark) was at BestBuy, we made a major change in our business model from doing commission-based sales to a "great price, no pressure" model. It meant we had a huge challenge to revamp our sales approach on the fly, without being able to pause business and train people.

We spent a lot of time on the road, observing how business was conducted. One of our key training principles for managers was: "Positioned to notice."

> One of our key training principles for managers was: "Positioned to notice."

To explain, when we went to a store, it was not uncommon for a manager to be in their office. They may have been doing useful company work on a computer, but they were not in a position to actively lead and support their teams on the sales floor.

Over time, we got rid of offices that were out of sight of where the action was really happening. Sometimes a physical solution is more effective than a whole lot of training sessions and reminders. (The Japanese have a term for this: "Poka Yoke." It means designing something so that it can only be done correctly. For example, most modern electrical plugs cannot be put in backward, but only the one correct way.)

On the other end of the spectrum of involvement, we would sometimes notice managers who were at cash registers ringing up customers. That may be regarded as a good thing—managers stepping in and doing customer-facing work. But again, that meant they were not positioned to notice what was going on across the whole sales floor.

This third "Enabling" dimension of the PREP Framework is extremely target rich. In our experience, no organization has yet to come close to running out of EXD opportunities here, not to mention the opportunities in the other dimensions.

4. *Performance Experiences in the PREP Framework*

The last piece of PREP is Performance experiences. The three other elements—Purpose, Relationship, and Enabling—all combine to allow employees to do their jobs. This last piece relates to expectations and outcomes. To be more specific:

- Establishing clear role expectations and performance metrics.
- Providing regular and constructive feedback on performance.
- Creating paths for career progression.
- Implementing fair and transparent reward and recognition programs.
- Clearly defining what is expected of new hires.
- Improving daily activities like being clear about goals in meetings.

Here's an example of how onboarding should not work. I (Mark) once worked for a famous retailer. (I've worked for several, but I'm being vague here to protect the guilty.) My wife was past her due date, and I was scheduled to start on a particular Monday. As it turned out, our daughter was born the Saturday before. I called my new boss, "Bob," to explain the situation and ask for a postponement of my start date. Bob not only refused, but he said I needed to come in earlier than planned on Monday because there was a union organizing campaign at one of the call centers.

When I arrived that Monday, I had an hour-long meeting with Bob. Then he stood up and announced that he was off to catch a plane. He was heading to the distribution center for the entire week.

I'm like: "OK, but how do I know what I'm supposed to be doing this week?"

"You're an experienced HR person, right? You know what to do."

"Yes I am, but this is a totally different company. I don't know your priorities or the systems you have. I don't know your ways of working or know anyone here."

"Here's the deal: If you do something wrong, I'll let you know, OK? Otherwise, assume everything's good. Bye."

Long story short, the job went downhill from there.

Part of the challenge when working with Performance experiences is what we might call "settling."

> We settle for somewhat/kind of clear role expectations because we're new to the job and we don't want to push back too hard on our new boss. Besides—this job description is not much worse than other ones we've had in our career.
>
> We settle for an hour-long annual performance review and even briefer quarterly updates because our boss is very busy. Besides, the reviews tend to be stilted, uncomfortable sessions and the sooner they're over, the better.
>
> We settle for no discussion about career paths. After all, it's never happened in any jobs we've had, and raising the topic creates awkward questions like: "Why are you asking?"

Of course, HR and other leaders have forever handled the "Performance" topics of performance metrics, career paths, recognition programs, and so on. Our point in bringing them up here is to say you don't need to go searching for projects that are candidates for employee experience design—they're what you deal with every day. Instead, it's a matter of applying the EXD mindset to the next project you tackle.

More ways to use the PREP Framework

We've found PREP to be useful in three situations:

> *You don't need to go searching for projects that are candidates for employee experience design—they're what you deal with every day.*

1. As we saw above, when you're in the midst of organizing all the experiences that relate to a project you're co-designing, PREP is a **logical and effective way to categorize them by type:** Purpose, Relationship, Enabling, and Performance.
2. Even before you embark on a project, it's also a **good way to communicate the full scope of EXD to other leaders.** It helps them to see that EXD is much broader than engagement surveys or perks. It covers the spectrum of experiences that shape how people feel and perform at work.
3. Finally, PREP can **help to design an EX opportunity**. For any challenge you tackle, the team can ask itself: "What aspect of our proposed solution relates to improving relationship experiences?" If you ask and answer those questions about all four dimensions of PREP, you can be confident that you've covered all the bases.

One more helpful framework for you to use: The "Know Think Suspect" workshop

We've covered the design brief and PREP Framework so far in this chapter, but we want to hook you up with one additional method for building a strong EXD function. It's called "Know Think Suspect," and it's so useful that you may end up saving time by referring to it as "KTS" with your colleagues. It's what we'll call it here.

It's particularly useful when you want to gather perspectives from a group, and it's tailor-made to use on your organization's leaders (though it works on others, too).

Let's assume that you're involved in the first Employee Experience Design effort at your organization. You didn't launch it with fanfare; instead, as we talked about in the last chapter, you gathered some key people who have a combination of open-mindedness, a willingness to pitch in, and influence. You have a design brief as outlined earlier in this chapter.

At any rate, you've called a meeting where people don't need to do any preparation, because you're going to ask them to look at a topic from three distinct perspectives.

At the heart of KTS are those three words, which we'll use with specific meanings as follows:

1. **Know.** This perspective is reserved for things that can be *clearly substantiated*. It includes things for which someone has a solid base of supporting data; where multiple people have conveyed the same information; or where people agree that the information is considered *proven and definitive*. An example: "We know that fewer than 20 employees have applied in the last year for an internship that we thought would be potentially very popular."
2. **Think.** This category of insights is not quite as solid as what's in the "Know" category—it refers to things that have a single data point, or something that's been personally witnessed. Yes, it's evidence, but it's going to need more validation before it can be firmly relied upon. Example: "It's because of the eligibility requirements that no one's applying. I spoke with one person who had been excited for the internship, but she said there were so many hoops to jump through that she gave up."
3. **Suspect.** This is the perspective of gut feelings and interpretations. They may be opinions based on many years of experience, but even so, they're unproven. Someone says: "I don't think it's the eligibility rules, because they're no worse than our other internships and those have done well. I'm pretty sure it's because we launched it in the dead of summer and we didn't follow up with any real awareness campaign."

Consider how powerful these three distinctions are: In any discussion on just about any organizational topic, you can now put viewpoints into one of these three buckets. You may well find that people adopt this framework to the point where it's just common language. Someone makes

> *In any discussion on just about any organizational topic, you can now put viewpoints into one of these three buckets.*

a statement and someone else goes: "Is that something you think, or just suspect?" An outsider might be puzzled by that question, but your team isn't. It's so much more useful than the typical language of: "That's just your opinion."

You heard in Chapter 6 about how KTS was used extensively when Haka House was challenged by an acquisition that expanded its operations by 200 percent. But let's now see how this framework might play out in your organization.

What happens in the KTS workshop

So, you have the leaders gathered in a room. Of course, they have some idea about the topic or they wouldn't have made time. Depending on your earlier conversations with them, you may choose to give them a little background on EXD. What won't work is to go into too much detail so that they feel like they're back in school. The sooner you can get to the KTS questions, the better.

You mention the design brief and the activities that have led to this point. You then give them an overview of the Double Diamond (which we cover in the next chapter). Again, it's not supposed to be a class about it, and you might not even mention much about all the concepts you now know. For example, their brains will explode if you start to lay on them Moments that Matter, Moments of Truth, the four parts of the PREP Framework, and the moving parts of the Double Diamond. Unless you have an audience of engineers who really like popping the hood and getting into the inner workings, just keep it conversational:

"So, as you know, we have the design brief that so far—subject to change—reads as follows:

> "How might we improve our non-health-insurance related benefits so that we don't increase our budget but can "spend smarter" and optimize the mix of benefits that employees value the most?"

> We have roughly two dozen interviews scheduled in the next two weeks with employees from several areas. We're focused on learning more about what we offer that they value, things we offer that could be improved, and what we're not offering that employees would be interested in.

Three Frameworks

We wanted to have this discussion today to answer any questions you have. Also, I'm interested in your thoughts about the following question: What do you anticipate people are going to say in our upcoming interviews?"

At this point, you give each person a pad of sticky notes and ask everyone to take maybe five minutes to jot down thoughts about the question you just asked. If you're getting some puzzled looks, you can model what you're hoping to get by giving an example: "For example, maybe you anticipate that people will push back and say: 'We need a larger benefits package to become competitive.' So just write that on the sticky note. Remember, these aren't yet solutions, so whatever people say is fair game for the moment. We're simply trying to anticipate what they'll say."

Notice that we did not define the three categories of Know, Think, and Suspect just yet. It's sometimes good to just get people engaged and writing their thoughts on the notepads. Otherwise, some people may slow down, trying to generate ideas and simultaneously categorize them with a method that's new to them.

If people are on a roll, then ask if the group would like to go for a little longer. When you see that "let's get moving" look, ask people to get into pairs. Now review the definitions of the "Know, Think, and Suspect" categories. It might take people a moment to process this new way of looking at comments, so it could be helpful to have a graphic where they can see each category defined. Ask them to spend around 15 minutes to group their individual stickies into a shared list consisting of the Know, Think, and Suspect buckets.

As people discuss each sticky note, there will inevitably be differences of opinion, and that's fine. But at least if you have the graphic up, they won't differ on what each category means. (At the back of this book, leave your email and we'll be happy to send you some graphics that we've used in KTS workshops.)

At this point, you'll have several pairs of people who have many stickies organized under the three categories, and maybe a fourth bunch where they couldn't decide or agree on the category. You don't want the meeting to drag, so it's best to finish by doing two things:

First, explain that you'll take all these stickies and create one document that combines and organizes them.

Second, a good way to wrap up this session is to ask each pair to spend a couple of minutes describing what they put under each of the three categories.

> *Having any EXD-related sessions end a bit early sends a subliminal message that these are not like other meetings—they're better.*

If possible, end the session earlier than it was scheduled to end. We all know how meetings usually drag on. Having any EXD-related sessions end a bit early sends a subliminal message that these are not like other meetings—they're better.

Then follow up with a document that combines *all* the notes; as we said in the last chapter, overlooking someone's ideas is a way to shut that person down from further participation. You can explain that you listed all the notes and then grouped them into themes. If a few notes defied categorizing, or they're too cryptic, you can indicate that.

At this point, you should have a feeling whether it makes sense to get the group together for further discussion, or whether it would be better to just send this report to the group and ask them for questions or comments. Either way, you've brought the leaders up to speed on the nature of the project, and you've involved them early in the process.

You've done one other thing: You have had them state their expectations about what the interviews will yield. That creates a baseline of expectations. Once you conduct those interviews, it's almost certain that the interviewees will come up with comments and ideas—and possibly the eventual solutions—that were not at all anticipated by the leaders.

> *That's the whole point of EXD: Leaders don't need to have all the answers, nor will they. Using a straightforward framework, we can co-design solutions, and we all benefit.*

Think how powerful this is: The leaders most likely were pretty sure they knew what their employees would say—but some comments were complete surprises that no one anticipated. That's the whole point of EXD: Leaders don't need to have all the answers, nor will they. Using a straightforward framework, we can co-design solutions, and we all benefit.

At this point, you've added the leaders' important voices to the project, and you've engaged them in the process. Again, consider this process flexible based on your specific situation. You may have a hard time convening many leaders in a meeting; that's not unusual. In that case, you might be able to get only a handful of them, so your event may look more like an informal conversation than a meeting. Maybe you only get one person—you work with what you have.

We've accomplished a lot in this chapter: You are now able to create a design brief, which provides a foundation for reaching consensus on what a specific project might look like. You know how to use the PREP Framework to identify a huge number of potential projects that would benefit from employee experience design; and you can hold a KTS workshop to engage leaders in what they think the EXD process will discover. Next, let's talk about a tool that's amazingly effective and central to just about any EXD project.

Chapter Summary

We looked in depth at the importance of design in Employee Experience Design—how it signifies intentionality and leads to positive user experiences.

The design brief is a mandatory starting point for any EXD project, laying out scope, goals, audience, budget, timeline, deliverables, and constraints to prevent "ready-fire-aim" approaches.

The minimum effective design brief uses the phrases "How might we ... so that ..." to encourage brainstorming solutions and explicitly link the project to organizational outcomes.

The PREP Framework breaks down employee experience into four key types, helping organizations to begin EXD efforts:

1. **Purpose** experiences: focuses on meaning, mission alignment, and impact of work (tying KPIs to mission, celebrating successes, volunteer opportunities).
2. **Relationship** experiences: pertains to interactions and connections among colleagues, managers, and teams (team building, fostering honest disagreement, Community Captains, "Radical Candor").

3. **Enabling** experiences: provides tools, resources, processes, and work environment for effective job performance ("progressive de-bottlenecking," physical workspaces, training, efficient onboarding).
4. **Performance** experiences: relates to expectations and outcomes (clear role expectations, feedback, career progression, recognition, clear new-hire expectations).

KTS is a framework that you can deliver in workshop form. It's powerful because it puts leaders in the shoes of employees in three ways:

1. **Know.** Things that can be *clearly substantiated* with a solid base of supporting data.
2. **Think.** Not quite as solid as what's in the "Know" category—things that have a single data point, or something that's been personally witnessed. It will need more validation before it can be firmly relied upon.
3. **Suspect.** Opinions, gut feelings, and interpretations. These can be useful but are unproven.

Once the EXD process has gathered employee perspectives, it can be eye-opening to compare those with what leaders earlier said they know, think, and suspect will be the case.

9

The Double Diamond

A Proven Design Method

As we said in Chapter 1, on one level, the concept of Employee Experience Design is so very simple: Design with, not for, your employees.

If you get that concept tattooed somewhere prominent so that you apply it regularly, you'll be ahead of most organizations. Our goal for this book is to support you in those efforts, by making it as easy as possible for you to get going with EXD projects. After all, we promised that EXD can mean less on your plate, not more.

One way to have less on your plate is to have a tested and proven way of approaching projects. We've already made progress in that direction: The PREP Framework lets you identify many promising areas for applying employee experience design. The design brief then gives you a structure for talking with others about what a project might look like and how it would benefit the organization.

You're now ready for the next step—equipping yourself with a surprisingly powerful tool.

Let's say you're a designer for a major company. Let's say that you have a whole staff of designers, even. Here's the problem: No matter how design oriented your company is, you have to deal with people who have no experience in design. Maybe the CEO has a finance background, and maybe the entire C-suite has no design background. How do you create a system that allows both designers and non-designers to look at a problem, discuss it, and make contributions to the solution?

That was the challenge facing the British Design Council in the early 2000s. They put together a team to come up with a universally understandable way to collaborate on a design process. They built upon work that had started as early as the 1960s, and the Council eventually created what they called the "Double Diamond Model."[1]

The Double Diamond is so powerful that it's been used by Apple, Sony, LEGO, Starbucks, Microsoft, major governments, and universities.

This isn't a history book, so let's get to the bottom line: The Double Diamond is so powerful that it's been used by Apple, Sony, LEGO, Starbucks, Microsoft, major governments, and universities.

Just think of the impression you'll make when someone asks you where this "diamond thing" came from and you can say: "Companies like Apple, Sony, LEGO, and Microsoft use it to help design their world-class products. It was made to be used by both designers and non-designers. In fact, that's the whole point of it." You just got their attention.

The whole idea of the Double Diamond is to come at a problem with divergent and convergent thinking—first expansive, then narrowing. It's a mechanism for exploring and defining problems without jumping to conclusions. It's also a model that allows for customizing to suit the situation. That's super important because sometimes you'll conduct employee

---

[1] https://www.designcouncil.org.uk/our-resources/the-double-diamond/history-of-the-double-diamond/

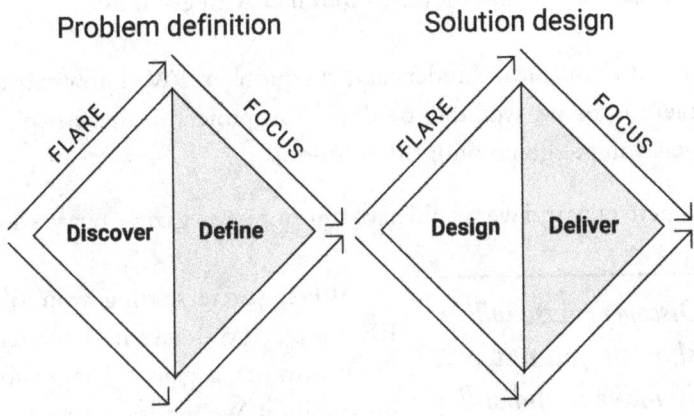

Figure 9.1 The Double Diamond method.

experience design by dealing with only a handful of employees, and other times it might be across your entire organization. Your tools must be able to adapt, and the Double Diamond does that.

It makes sense to call it a Double Diamond if you look at the diagram in Figure 9.1. Looking at it from left to right, you go wide and then narrow, then wide and again narrow.

The Double Diamond consists of four phases: Discover, Define, Design, and Deliver. Let's look at each phase in detail.

Phase 1: Discover (or Discovery)

One of the most common mistakes you can make when doing Employee Experience Design in general—and in using the Double Diamond in particular—is to bypass the foundational steps and jump right to solutions. The problem with that is your judgment can never be better than your information.

We talked in Chapter 2 about how work gets done in typical, average organizations. A project appears on our radar, and it often seems to be late from the outset because someone needs a deliverable, pronto. We have no framework like a Double Diamond, so we have a bias toward things that look like progress. If someone suggests that we first take the time to understand the problem deeply, they are often met with eye rolls:

> "What do you mean 'understand the problem'? We know what the problem is, or we wouldn't be doing this project in the first place! I suggest you get going with the solution!"

> "In a perfect world we would have time for navel gazing, but we don't."

The Discover phase will be as short as you can possibly make it and still come away with the facts you need.

When you're starting your very first EXD project, you have no track record to show how it's a game changer for your organization. We get it. At the same time, we know how important the Discovery phase is to the Double Diamond and to a good outcome. That's why it may help to explain again to people that this is the process that legendary companies like Apple and Microsoft use to design new products, and they're under world-class pressure to deliver quickly. You can also stress that the Discovery phase will be as short as you can possibly make it and still come away with the facts you need.

And you do need those facts. As we discussed in Chapter 2, when organizations across America were under pressure to adopt DEI initiatives in the wake of the George Floyd murder, it was common for leaders to announce a program without ever having asked their Black employees for input. If they had spent the time on the Discovery phase, they might have quickly realized what issues and solutions would work best for their situation.

The Discovery phase is characterized by "flare thinking," where your goal is to go wide. Everyone knows about the typical brainstorming sessions in organizations—usually done for solutions. Here, what we want to do is take a similar nonjudgmental approach, but we're focused on gathering as many facts and details about what the problem is in the first place. We want to be highly confident that we know what the specific problem is.

Just within the Discovery phase, you have many tools and options to choose from to uncover facts and details you can use:

User Research

This category includes doing surveys, focus groups, and some types of data analysis. The goal is to understand users' needs, behaviors, and pain points. For example, you might find that in the last 12 months, literally only 3 people have accessed the old 1.0 version of the policy you're revamping, when on average, policies get hundreds of views in a year. That becomes a data point either indicating disinterest or maybe just that everyone is unaware of the policy in the first place.

Interviews

After you've done surveys and focus groups, it may be helpful to sit down with a few hand-picked people to really understand their perspectives, experiences, and feelings in more detail. These interviews can range from structured Q&A sessions all the way to a chat over coffee, depending on what you're after and what works best for the interviewee. If you take the time to develop rapport with the person, you may break through a barrier and suddenly get a wealth of useful perspectives from that person. Of course, this involves making it clear that it's safe to talk with you—what they say will not come back to bite them. The interview in Chapter 6 is a great example of using this approach.

Observation

Also sometimes known as "shadowing," this can be a powerful tool for understanding how things actually work—or don't work. People are likely to be happy to have you observe them, as long as you're careful to explain that you're not monitoring or judging them, but instead you're interested in all the hoops they have to jump through in order to do their jobs. When you also explain that you're focused on improving the employee experience, you may have some enthusiastic participants.

Desk Research

This is research you can do without involving others. AI has advanced to the point that some systems have literally digested the entire internet. Of course, the internet also contains a lot of junk, but even so, it's becoming easier to ask some complicated questions and get useful answers.

Journey Mapping

This is a concept borrowed from customer-experience and user-experience mapping, and it's both interesting and useful. What you do is break down an experience into granular, separate chunks and then you classify those chunks.

For example, let's say your organization makes a big deal about how it's a great place to work in part because of the tuition reimbursement policy it has for employees. The C-suite is proud of this benefit, but the latest surveys indicate that there's a lot of negativity around the tuition reimbursement policy. It's not mentioned much at all, and when it is, it's a negative.

Typical organizations might chalk it up by saying: "You can't please everyone" or "They just don't appreciate all we do for them." Because you understand the power of EXD, you decide to dig deeper into what's going on with tuition reimbursement.

The survey results give you a clue about the issues, with comments like: "The portal sucks" and "It's impossible to complete the process." But exactly what sucks, and what makes it impossible?

There are many variations to a journey map, but let's talk about a simple one where you list granular elements from top to bottom, and next to each element you indicate what happened along the journey step and also one of three states: Calm, Puzzled, or Frustrated. (Or you might come up with other descriptors that better suit your needs.)

It can be in a simple spreadsheet and starts out looking like what you see in Figure 9.2. (If you can read the spreadsheet on your device, great. If not, we'll discuss the steps after Figure 9.2.)

The Double Diamond 115

The Journey Map

	ACTION I TAKE	RESULT I GET	STATE
01	I enter "tuition reimbursement" in the search box on the company intranet.	No results.	Puzzled
02	I send a message to Support asking why "tuition reimbursement" is not there.	Don't hear back.	Frustrated
03	I send another message to Support two days later.	Am told it's findable not under "tuition reimbursement" but under "Lifelong Learning Benefit."	Calm
04	I find the link for Lifelong Learning Benefit and get to the login screen.	It asks for my "Account Number" with no explanation. What account number? My employee ID? My federal loan account number? Bank account for reimbursement? Something else?	Frustrated
05	I contact Support.	They don't know, but they say I need to call a different number because this benefit is administered by a third party.	Frustrated
06	I call the outside number.	They said if I'm a first-time user of the system I need to create an account with the provider, and that was in a FAQ way lower down on the screen.	Frustrated
07	I create an account.	I'm finally inside the portal.	Calm
08	I look around inside the portal. I see they have lots of information on different loan types.	They use language about federal loan types that does not match what I'm used to seeing.	Puzzled
09	I want to know what I should do next.	I go to the "Support" section and see a very meager FAQ. There is nothing for "first-time users" or "Take a tour" or anything like that.	Frustrated

Figure 9.2 The start of a journey map.

Now comes the interesting part. By "granular element," we mean every little thing that happens or does not happen when people expect it to.

Let's now try to navigate the tuition reimbursement process.

1. I enter "tuition reimbursement" in the search box on the company intranet.
   No results.
   Puzzled.
2. I send a message to Support asking why "tuition reimbursement" is not there.
   Don't hear back.
   Frustrated.
3. I send another message to Support two days later.
   Am told it's findable not under "tuition reimbursement" but under "Lifelong Learning Benefit."
   Calm.
4. I find the link for Lifelong Learning Benefit and get to the login screen.
   It asks for my "Account Number" with no explanation. What account number? My employee ID? My federal loan account number? Bank account for reimbursement? Something else?
   Frustrated.
5. I contact Support.
   They don't know, but they say I need to call a different number because this benefit is administered by a third party.
   Frustrated.
6. I call the outside number.
   They said if I'm a first-time user of the system, I need to create an account with the provider, and that was in a FAQ way lower down on the screen.
   Frustrated.
7. I create an account.
   I'm finally inside the portal.
   Calm.

8. I look around inside the portal.
   I see they have lots of information on different loan types. They use language about federal loan types that does not match what I'm used to seeing.
   Puzzled.
9. I want to know what I should do next.
   I go to the "Support" section and see a very meager FAQ. There is nothing for "first-time users" or "Take a tour" or anything like that.
   Frustrated.

You get the idea. It's an example of a system that, on one level is up and working, but on another level is definitely not user friendly. Almost every step presents friction for the user. Most likely the vendor supplying this system sees no issues, saying: "We get very few complaints." If I as a user am completely frustrated by this third-party system, I probably won't waste even more of my time to complain, and wouldn't even know how to lodge a complaint.

From the C-suite's perspective, we offer this great reimbursement benefit, and few people take advantage of it; we just hear low-level grousing. But from the EXD perspective, this is a project that's ripe for co-designing an improved 2.0 version. In fact, just doing the journey map goes a long way toward knowing exactly what the bottlenecks are.

Just doing the journey map goes a long way toward knowing exactly what the bottlenecks are.

Someone might push back and say: "Hey, we have no control over the third-party administrator of this benefit. Are you suggesting that we rip them out and go with someone else, or battle to get their system overhauled?"

We would reply that at the moment, we're in the Discovery phase. We're uncovering granular, actionable insights into what is working and not working. Later there will be time to come up with all kinds of possible solutions, ranging from going with someone else; revamping the system; simply providing a helpful video walkthrough; creating an on-demand webinar about the program; greatly expanding the FAQ and making it prominent; and so on.

Another type of mapping (among many) is "empathy mapping" where the focus is more on users' thoughts, feelings, statements, and other actions. Where journey mapping might fit best with understanding how systems and people interact, empathy mapping could be more appropriate when understanding how policies are received by employees.

Market and Competitor Analysis

We talked in Chapter 5 about how we all have consumer-grade expectations for how things should work, and that the employee experience can often be a disappointment in comparison. One aspect of this has to do with market and competitor analysis. We're not referring to your product-development folks keeping on top of the marketplace and the latest features from competitors. Instead, we mean the marketplace for talent.

Keeping with our example above about tuition reimbursement, what comprehensive information do we have about what other organizations in our space are doing, relating to tuition reimbursement? It's not unusual for our employees—and also the candidates we interview—to be much more aware than the leadership of an organization, relating to the current job market. They may be interviewing at several of our competitors, and the most-qualified candidates are being pitched with the best those organizations have to offer.

In addition to whatever we may find online in the Discovery phase, we can make a point of regularly asking employees and candidates for information on the job market. Even if an employee of ours has no intention of interviewing elsewhere at the moment, that person has friends who may be actively interviewing. If we tell people that we'd like this information in order to make sure that we're competitive, they may be eager to help.

Another source of information is known as "mystery shopping." It's where an organization hires companies whose business it is to have representatives who pretend to be customers. This is not corporate espionage because it does not focus on uncovering secrets; only on understanding the entire consumer experience of a competitor and documenting it. It may well be that your organization has been mystery-shopped. Some companies hire mystery shoppers to go through their own buying processes, as a way to get unbiased observations.

It's Called Discovery for a Reason It's a common human tendency to suffer from "confirmation bias" where we look for facts and other information to support our existing opinions. But part of the power of the Discovery phase done correctly is to uncover information that was previously unknown to us. Therefore, at this phase, it's useful to become an information magnet that attracts pieces from many directions. There will be time to sort it all out later.

Dig Deeply for Root Causes In Chapter 5, we talked about how a colleague of ours was tasked with finding a new Applicant Tracking System, when the problem wasn't that system at all; it was that managers perceived the caliber of the candidates being sourced as poor. Root-cause analysis is time well spent, because it can help you to avoid spending time on projects that ultimately won't solve the problem—only fixing the root cause will do that.

Root-cause analysis is time well spent, because it can help you to avoid spending time on projects that ultimately won't solve the problem—only fixing the root cause will do that.

One famous method for doing root-cause analysis is called the "5 Whys" technique, developed by the founder of what later became Toyota Motor Company.[2] It involves asking "why" multiple times as follows:

1. Why did our overall employee satisfaction numbers drop this month?
   Because the biggest drop occurred in our employee engagement score; the other elements of satisfaction were relatively steady.
2. Why did employee engagement drop?
   Because the Western Region's numbers went down the most, by far.
3. Why is the Western Region's engagement so low?
   Because we consolidated our call centers and the Western Region had to switch to "all hands on deck" for weeks until we had staffing sorted out.

---

[2] https://oncpracticemanagement.com/issues/2021/april-2021-vol-11-no-4/2253:using-the-5-whys-method-to-identify-and-solve-problems

Now maybe we stop at three Whys if there are no deeper causes that our exploration turns up—there is no magic to asking "why" literally five times. The point is to not accept the first answer, but to keep searching for underlying causes until there's agreement that we've reached the fundamental cause.

Wide Versus Narrow Discovery

The Double Diamond is highly flexible. With all the ways we listed above to conduct discovery, it might seem that the process will take months. The length of time depends on the scope of what you're trying to achieve. If your goal is to do more of a strategic overview of potential areas for improvement in employee experience, you might use many of these techniques. It could be worth the effort because you'll be using the insights you gain on many sub-projects.

Then again, you might do narrow discovery when you have in mind a specific area of employee experience to explore in more depth. If that tuition reimbursement policy revamp is on your plate, you'll be dealing with a fraction of your employee base. Though you might use several of the methods above, discovery might be relatively quick.

Phase 2: Define

Let's say we've gathered a pile of information from the Discovery phase. The Define phase is the second half of that first diamond, and it involves making sense of what we just gathered.

Just as the Discovery phase involved what you might call "flare thinking"—you're purposefully casting a wide net—now you want to have "focus thinking" where the puzzle pieces begin to come together.

It's useful to keep in mind that most of what you gathered in the Discovery phase will fall into the following three categories:

1. **Data.** We're talking about raw numbers, like survey scores, number of people participating in something, costs, length of time something goes on for, and the like.
2. **Information.** You know what information is, but here we're referring to comparing one thing to another. It's critical to have data and facts

like raw survey scores from around the country, but those numbers alone don't mean much. You start to get useful information when you compare numbers: Our average engagement score, the slowest and fastest time for tuition reimbursement to happen, the job acceptance rate of our candidates, and so on.

3. **Insights.** Now we're talking. Here's where we might do some data mining and see things that the data and information don't quite show on their own. If we're slicing the data in new ways, we might start to see trends. Suddenly what we're looking at are not "lagging indicators" of what happened in the past, but "leading indicators" of what's coming up. In Chapter 12 on Metrics, you're in for a treat with some stories, plus tools you can use in your own organization.

> *Suddenly what we're looking at are not "lagging indicators" of what happened in the past, but "leading indicators" of what's coming up.*

Another way to look at this phase is first we gather our findings, which could be quantitative, qualitative, or both; then our job is to glean insights and narrow them down to the problem we're trying to solve.

AI is getting pretty good at deriving insights from tons of data; it could be worth a try. It's now possible to train an AI agent on your own data, while not allowing it to be used outside of your organization. These systems have become so good, so fast that the question becomes: *Why wouldn't we see what we can learn from AI?*

While you're sifting and sorting that pile of material, some of it will be quantitative, like data/information/insights, but you'll also have qualitative elements like survey comments, social media posts, Glassdoor reviews, and so on. How do all these things fit together?

Don't Stop with One Observation

Just as the 5 Whys can be useful for finding root causes, think of the Define phase as the "5 Maybes": Keep going until you have more than one possible explanation for what you found during Discovery.

Using our tuition reimbursement example, we might start to jot some notes along the following lines:

1. Maybe people don't know about the benefit.
   A. Find out when was the last time we talked about tuition reimbursement.
2. Maybe people are aware of the program, but they think our guidelines don't cover the most popular loan types.
   A. What are the most popular loan types?
   B. Find out from our administrator the distribution of loan types our people are getting reimbursed for.
   C. Is there a discrepancy that might indicate a problem?
3. Maybe the portal makes it too hard to use, so people either give up or think *I'll come back to it later* and never do.
   A. Can we get data on which data fields in the portal are the point where most people abandon the process?
4. Maybe people think the policy cannot benefit them because their loans were taken out by parents (even though we will reimburse if it was for the benefit of our employee).
   A. Do a follow-up survey via email that asks this specific question.

Notice how the deeper we dig, the more follow-up actions we have. That's an important feature of the Double Diamond: **You don't necessarily "finish" a phase like Discovery and move on.** These phases in reality become loops: We got pretty far in Discovery and moved to Define but then circled back as we realized we could use more data.

Involve Others—Carefully

In this process of developing hypotheses or Maybes, it's a good idea to involve others to help. They may see trends and have questions that didn't occur to you, and vice versa. This is an interesting phase where it feels good to find a previously overlooked clue, follow it, and potentially uncover an underlying problem nobody thought about.

It's worth choosing carefully the people you involve at this stage. Let's assume this is your first effort at employee experience design. If the CEO and the rest of the C-suite are enthusiastic about EXD then you've just won the lottery. You can move ahead quickly. It's more likely that many people in your organization have never heard of EXD, and if they have, their opinion involves several of the misconceptions we covered in Chapter 2. What now?

You can do two things: First, don't announce that there's this amazing new approach known as Employee Experience Design. That's putting a target on it for people to shoot at. They may immediately do what we said in Chapter 2—dismiss it as another fad; say they tried it and it doesn't work; and so on. You're better off just implementing elements of EXD, like getting people together to do the Discovery phase and the Design phase of the Double Diamond.

But doesn't that put a label on things, too? It's just an individual tool and not the whole ecosystem of EXD; besides you can mention all the heavyweights who use the Double Diamond. But even with that tool, you can always eliminate labels like "Discovery Phase" and just talk about gathering information, organizing it, and so on.

The second thing that increases the odds of success is to think about who the right influencers within your organization might be. There are always some people who are more open-minded than others and who relish any opportunity to get incrementally better. They might be senior leaders but also could be line managers or even individual contributors. Of course, it's great if you can enlist people who are higher in the organization, but you just need to work with what you have.

The best way to approach these people is with an attitude of how they'd be great on the project that's come up. You have some really interesting approaches that you've been reading about and that have been successful at companies like Airbnb, Patagonia, and others, and you'd love to get their help. Some will be too busy, but others may be more than happy to improve how things get done.

Look for Discrepancies

Information analysts do this all the time. For example, let's say you're on a project where you want to increase the number of employees who participate in volunteering activities through the organization. One of your team members is a developer and begins to snoop around the analytics behind the volunteering webpages.

Extremely few organizations make full use of web analytics. Usually the data is plentiful, but the analysis stops at primitive measures like "number of visitors" and "time on page." This can be a major area for potential insights.

Anyhow, your smart developer notices an interesting discrepancy. There's a measure called "bounce rate" which is defined as follows: If you land on a page and then leave the site without interacting with the page or visiting other pages, that's a bounce. It happens to some degree on pretty much all pages, but what's interesting are discrepancies: Why is it that our average bounce rate is 22 percent, but the bounce rate for our tuition reimbursement page is more than double, at 52 percent? Oh, and why is it that the bounce rate for people viewing our page using the Chrome browser is about 31 percent, but people using Apple's Safari browser is literally 100 percent?

Someone looking just at overall averages may see numbers like 22 percent and 31 percent and may think *There's nothing here—we're more or less average,* when only if you dig into the granular data can you uncover the problems.

This sort of thing happens all the time, and it's often a clue that a page is broken for people who use certain cell phones or certain browsers to view the content. It's great to find these discrepancies because the fix is often easy and often relates to many pages on your site. Then you can get benefits across the organization because now your site is finally accessible for another slice of your population.

Look for Themes or Patterns

These might be found deep into quantitative "hard" data, but it's also there for the spotting without having to crunch a lot of numbers. For example, let's say that leadership is getting frustrated that some of the most expensive benefits are not getting the use we predicted. It's becoming harder to justify the expense in some cases.

In this Define phase, we might have to do a lot of digging, thinking, discussing, and note-taking before we start to see things. One highly successful person calls it "circling the table." He spreads out onto a big table all the information he has on a topic and looks it over. He gets up and maybe rearranges some of the reports and other material into groupings that seem logical. He goes out for a cup of coffee and then comes back with fresher eyes to look at the assembled stuff again.

So, as you're circling the table with what you know about this benefits-use challenge, one morning you look at the pile again and realize that you don't have anything about email. In other words, you know that Comms created emails for the launch of each benefit; how did those emails perform? How many were there? What did they say?

This is where you might discover one or more insights:

We had three separate benefit announcements and each of these campaigns involved four emails—except one of the campaigns was seven emails. Did the longer campaign result in more engagement by employees?... It turns out yes! We seem to have little engagement bumps after emails, so why are we stopping them at four?

We announced these three separate benefits and one of them has particularly low engagement. Wait—we dropped that announcement in the week between Christmas and New Years. Could it be that fewer people read our emails around holidays and even the ones who do are distracted? Might that mean we just need to make announcements during slower times, or at least do a second mini launch during slower times?

You pull on one thread and it leads you to another. You notice something, which makes you need to get more information, which allows you to generate a new "Maybe." Employee Experience Design definitely does not happen in a straight line.

Sometimes this kind of digging has been worth a fortune to companies. In Chapter 3, we mentioned how the odor eliminator, Febreze, was created somewhat by accident. Long story short, after Procter & Gamble launched the product at great cost and with much fanfare—it began to look like a dud. The company was about to lose an enormous amount of money—and the team members were about to lose their jobs—when a guy decided to take home some video. It was filmed by researchers who went into people's homes to see how they used the product. He discovered that people felt good when they could see the result of their cleaning efforts. The problem was that the early Febreze was unscented! People weren't feeling so special about the absence of something. When they added a scent to Febreze, sales skyrocketed.[3] And it was because a curious researcher dug deeper into the data and saw things that you could not see unless you did that digging.

Consider Creating Personas

Some organizations find it useful to take what data and information they've gathered and create personas where applicable. Personas are a way to make the information come alive, in a sense. They can become a common reference point across teams and sometimes form the basis for discussions about what matters most to different user segments.

Create a Problem Statement

In Chapter 8, we talked about the power of creating a design brief. It helps to get everyone on the same page and to reach agreement about what outcome we're seeking and how it benefits the organization.

That brief is typically done before you dive into the Double Diamond. By the time you're in the Define phase of the Double Diamond, you have lots of data and information, and even some insights. It's time to think about creating a problem statement.

John Dewey, the American philosopher, said: "A problem well stated is a problem half solved."[4] By spending a relatively short time on being highly specific about the problem, you can avoid dead ends and wasted effort down the line.

You can think of a design brief as the desired state and the problem statement as the current state. The benefit of a problem statement is it is another forcing mechanism to get everyone on the same page. In Chapter 11 in our conversation with Melanie Rosenwasser, you'll hear how she used a problem statement. Without this statement, it's easy for discussions to become abstract and not grounded in facts.

---

[3] Duhigg, Charles. *The Power of Habit: Why We Do What We Do in Life and Business.* New York: Random House Trade Paperbacks, 2023, p. 55.
[4] https://plato.stanford.edu/entries/dewey/

Earlier, we used leadership training when discussing the design brief. Before the problem statement, people might say things along the lines of:

> "I don't see a problem here."
> Someone else says: "What do you mean you 'don't see a problem'? I wouldn't be surprised if our leadership scores have actually gone down."

You couldn't do the problem statement before now, because only now do you have the information and full evidence to formulate a description of the problem.

We used the following design brief in Chapter 8:

> "How might we design a leadership program so that it not only helps people to grow and develop, but will also help them to take ownership and feel valued?"

If we look over our assembled material from the Discover phase, and the sense we've made of it in the Define phase, we might now create a problem statement.

That statement should have at least two components:

1. A succinct statement of the problem, along with the main evidence we have to support it; and
2. Another succinct statement of how we will define and measure success.

Here's what we might come up with as our 1.0 version:

We have conducted three leadership programs in the last 30 months. The baseline survey scores from employees about their managers have hardly moved, and scores from the leadership team have slightly decreased compared to baseline on questions relating to taking ownership and feeling valued. In addition, there is a trend in leadership survey comments about the "time we're wasting" on these programs and "probably negative ROI."

We will measure success when our 360-degree evaluation indicates statistically significant improvements on overall leadership scores.

Please note how the problem statement says **nothing about how the problem will be addressed**; that comes later. For now, we need to help people focus only on what the problem is, and when we'll know that we have solved it.

Some organizations create elaborate problem statements that include target dates, affected stakeholders, consequences of inaction, what knowledge gaps we have, and so on. Those elements are worth considering, but we think what's really key is to **define the current problem as factually and succinctly as we can, and state how we'll know that we've solved the problem.**

Shoot for a minimum viable product that gets done quickly, rather than the perfect version that never happens because people are wordsmithing it to death.

Remember that like with pretty much everything in Employee Experience Design, you should shoot for a minimum viable product that gets done quickly, rather than the perfect version that never happens because people are wordsmithing it to death. You can always iterate when you circulate this statement to people you want to involve. They may have useful input and even some other data to consider.

Phase 3: Design

We just finished with the two parts of the first diamond, which combined to be the Problem Definition. This third phase gets us into the second diamond, which is Solution Design. As you know from your own personal experience, many people jump to this step without doing the Discover and Define phases. In one sense, they can't be blamed for not knowing that the Double Diamond exists, never mind how some of the best companies on the planet regularly use it.

Well, you know about it. You also know that it's a mistake to design solutions without having gathered facts and information about what's really going on.

It's also a mistake to not analyze all that material and come up with a crisp problem statement. Now comes a really interesting part of the design effort. In a way it's at the heart of designing with and not for employees.

Of course, you've been involved in many brainstorming sessions. You also have probably walked away from some of them feeling less than satisfied. Brainstorming can be done poorly in a whole lot of ways:

- One or two people dominate the discussion.
- All participants' ideas are not honored because some ideas get written out in detail while other people's ideas get a word or two on the flip chart, or don't even make it to the flip chart.
- Someone hijacks the discussion and takes it away from idea generation to some other topic. People may or may not feel like they can bring it back to the topic at hand.
- Someone starts to evaluate ideas as they are mentioned, instead of letting the ideas get noted and saving the evaluation until later. This usually happens multiple times.
- Someone with power decides that we've had enough of this brainstorming stuff and cuts short the session, even though other people were on a roll.
- The "scribe" starts to tire, and either becomes illegible and cryptic (if this is being done in person) or starts to not be very good at capturing ideas as time goes on.

Does this sound familiar? You probably have even more ways that brainstorming sessions have run into a ditch.

The thing about the Design phase is it's more than just a brainstorming session. Brainstorming is an excellent tool, but it needs to be done correctly and should be part of a larger design effort.

Given how common it is to have brainstorming sessions, let's first give you our two cents on how they should be conducted. First, the best sessions happen when there is both a facilitator and a scribe. The best facilitator is very often not the person in the room with the highest rank; ideally it's someone who's good at running meetings. But this is key: Whoever is the Big Dog in the room needs to give the facilitator the authority to run the meeting. In other words, for the 60 or 90 minutes that the session lasts, the facilitator needs to be the boss. That means they can shut down the Big Dog if that person starts to dominate things.

We get it: Many organizations have bosses who are control freaks, and they will cede control to no one for any reason. If you're in that kind of organization, we feel for you. But sometimes miracles happen, and it's possible to run meetings where the facilitator does have the ability to be respectful but firm. (We'll give you a workaround in a moment.)

The best situation is where an experienced facilitator runs the session. That solves several of the problems we listed above:

- When someone starts to dominate, the facilitator will interrupt to ask the scribe to note that person's issues on a "Parking Lot" document for further discussion later and will then bring the discussion back to the group.
- The facilitator will make sure that the scribe is noting ideas with consistent detail and will correct them if necessary.
- It's worth noting that the facilitator should not be the scribe! It's enough to be choreographing the session without also being responsible for writing everything down. These are two jobs for two people.
- Someone who hijacks the discussion gets shut down politely by having the issue noted on the Parking Lot list of other topics to address. If the hijacking involved going back to an earlier discussion, that too is stopped by making a note on the Parking Lot.
- The facilitator shuts down any evaluation of ideas during brainstorming, pointing out that there will be plenty of time later for that.
- The facilitator is militant about time. They get agreement before the meeting or at its outset about how much time will be devoted to each agenda point. Then the meeting starts *on time*, ends *on time*, and each agenda point gets its allotment of time. The only occasion when the time budget is violated is when the group agrees to an adjustment. (This single discipline will vastly improve meetings and leave participants wondering why all their meetings can't be run this way.)

- The facilitator should be a master at nonverbal communication. The good ones know when someone was just shut down by another, more-powerful person—and they jump in to invite the shut-down person to participate.

It's a sight to behold when an experienced facilitator runs a meeting, and we're here to tell you that it can happen. These people do exist, and even the Big Dogs usually realize that meetings go really well when that facilitator runs them.

Let's say you don't have such a person, but you do have the dominating types in abundance. What you do is break up the sessions. Have a main session where some of the power dynamics are evident, and then hold separate sessions with smaller groups, ideally consisting of people who feel freer to express their opinions.

Get Ideas over Time

An issue with brainstorming sessions is they tend to be one single session that's laden with the various issues we mentioned. Even if you solve them with a great facilitator, a long brainstorming session can become tedious. A single session also does not allow people's subconscious minds to work on the topics while they're taking a walk, driving home, or sleeping on it.

Sometimes you can have the best of both worlds. Hold the brainstorming session but leave the door open to further ideas. One thing I (Samantha) have done that's highly effective is I'll post a question in a public place, asking for feedback. Maybe it's a lunchroom, or a note on a Slack channel. I'll ask for feedback and give a deadline that's a few days away. If the list is in person, then I make sure some sticky notes and pens are nearby. People can jot an idea and put it on the sheet devoted to that idea. (There may be several sheets.)

People like this kind of interaction, where they're being asked for their opinions and they have time to think about what they want to say. This very act is a way of designing with and not for employees. Just make sure that if you create an online document from all the sticky notes, that you list *all of the ideas*. If you omit my ideas, the next time you want me to participate, I'll just walk on by.

Design with MVP in Mind

We mentioned the concept of Minimum Viable Product in Chapter 5. It's incredibly valuable to focus on MVP for two reasons: It relieves you from trying to build the Taj Mahal on your first try; and it speeds up the whole process.

It may be that some of the brainstormed ideas are detailed enough that they're practically an MVP already. Others may take more work. Either way, your next step is to sift and sort the list of ideas until you end up with a very small number that you'd like to work on. The other ideas don't get trashed; they're just maybe not right for the 1.0 version. You should not get bogged down at this phase—remember that you'll be iterating and it's crucial to just get going, even with a small part of the overall task.

> *Someone floats the idea but at that point—when it was just born—the idea is helpless, powerless, and can easily die.*

Once we participated in a planning session run by a professional facilitator. In today's dollars, he charged more than $6,000 per day for his services. He was careful to say at the outset that in his experience, there are what he called "baby ideas." Someone floats the idea but at that point—when it was just born—the idea is helpless, powerless, and can easily die. It's only when people respect these beginnings and allow some of them to grow in strength that they start to really flourish. Under the right circumstances, they can become powerful.

It's worth keeping that concept in mind when deciding which handful of ideas to run with. You can't work on them all, but sometimes it's worth nurturing some unusual ones to see how they develop.

One way to figure out which ideas to go with is to determine what your criteria are and then rate the semi-finalist ideas against those criteria. Here's another time when co-designing with your employees can help: They may suggest rating criteria that you never considered. Another great way to guide your decision-making is to have a representative group take a vote (preferably on paper, to avoid group dynamics of votes being influenced). This whole winnowing process can be difficult, but collaborating with those hand-picked other people makes it less so.

Test Like You're Wrong

Let's say you feel like you know the idea to run with. Keep that Minimum Viable Product concept in mind and create a rough prototype. It's a big step when you finally have something that mostly covers all the bases—something you can step back and look at.

By this point, you (or whoever is running the project) may be too close to have much objectivity, so once again you turn to others for opinions. As we said before, the quality of what you hear back depends on how you frame the question. If it's an expectant: "So, what do you think!" then you're telegraphing that you want a positive response. Some people may be honest with you, but you'll get more honesty if you invite it: "Here's our first version; what do you like about it and how would you improve it?" That statement is good because it binds the person to suggest improvements instead of merely saying: "That doesn't work for me."

Sometimes the project you're working on has a comparatively low downside; even after you've announced the results, it won't be a disaster to make changes. Other projects may have higher consequences if you get something wrong. For those cases, consider Red Teaming.

The concept goes back to the 1800s and has been called lots of things, but Red Team is the modern label. Let's say you have people who design something and then you ask them for the downsides. They may be able to state a few of them. But what if you had an entirely different group of people whose job it was to poke holes in a proposal? They're not being mean or negative; they're just stepping back and actively trying to find alternative interpretations for something. It's specifically asking people to play "devil's advocate."

Though it can be a little disconcerting to ask for such an analysis, consider the benefits: At worst, someone finds a flaw that you didn't see, and you can try to fix it before launching. At best, no one comes up with issues, and you have that much more confidence in your team's work product.

Phase 4: Deliver

You've put so much methodical thought and effort into the three previous phases of Discover, Define, and Design, that now you get to enjoy the fruits of your labor with Deliver.

That is not to say that you're "Done" of course! EXD is all about iterating. But you do finally get to show the world what the cross-organizational team has been working on.

If possible, the messaging around the delivery should include two elements: First, that this is a pilot, and we wanted to get something out, to see if we're heading in the right direction. Second, we invite people to give us their honest thoughts and especially their suggestions for improvement.

It really is true that "you don't learn until you ship." Here's an example: As I (Mark) mentioned earlier, at Airbnb we fostered the goal of "Belong Anywhere." To that end, we had a project of designing workspaces in our Portland office. Our team came up with the concept that employees would not have assigned desks but rather places to store belongings and recharge laptops. They then could "belong anywhere" and move around based on their needs. They could opt for a quiet library setting, a busier area that felt like a friend's backyard gathering, or a large kitchen table for group meetings. Many people have different favorite zones at home, after all.

When we launched, initially it was a complete free-for-all. After receiving a lot of employee feedback, it became clear that people felt like we had built a city with no neighborhoods. Employees were overwhelmed and lost; they belonged anywhere, but also nowhere!

Progress doesn't happen in a straight line. Our 1.0 version got us over the horizon; once we got there, we could see things that were not visible when we started.

We made some small changes and created those neighborhoods so people could congregate with their team members. They had spaces where they knew they could find people instead of each day being a random distribution. It wasn't too hard to make these changes, driven by employee feedback, but they didn't come to light until after the 1.0 version shipped. A cynic might point and say: "Ha! So, your whole 'co-design' thing failed from the outset, right?" We would say: "No, it's just that progress doesn't happen in a straight line. Our 1.0 version got us over the horizon; once we got there, we could see things that were not visible when we started, so we made course corrections." After a few adjustments, this workspace setup became incredibly successful.

Keep in Mind

Don't get the wrong idea about the concept of iterating. It doesn't mean that you're in the movie, *Groundhog Day*, where you live the same day over and over. At some point when you and your colleagues feel like you're done, then you're done. Get that dopamine fix from putting a big check mark next to the project. But of course, when circumstances change, then all "done" projects become candidates for review; that's always been real life.

It's also important to know that the Double Diamond doesn't have to take a super long time to do—depending on the project, you could complete it in a few days, or a few weeks. Maybe you objectively have a crystal-clear sense of the problem; you also have comprehensive information to support the problem statement and you have agreement on the design brief. In that case, you're done with the first diamond of Discover/Define and you can focus on the second diamond of Design/Deliver.

Then again, you may find that the longest piece of all is the Discover phase because in your particular organization, it takes a long time to conduct all the 1:1 interviews you need.

It's all good. We hope you see how powerful even just a part of the Double Diamond might be for your organization. And we're not done: In the next chapter we have another great framework we've used to help you design *with* employees.

Chapter Summary

The Double Diamond is a surprisingly powerful, universally understandable design tool used by major companies (Apple, Sony, LEGO, Microsoft) to collaborate on design processes.

It operates on the principle of divergent and convergent thinking ("flare" and "focus") across four phases: Discover, Define, Design, and Deliver.

- Phase 1: **Discover** involves wide, nonjudgmental gathering of facts and details about the problem, using tools like user research, interviews, observation, desk research, journey mapping, and market/competitor analysis.
- Phase 2: **Define** focuses on making sense of the gathered information, moving from raw data to comparative information and deeper insights, often involving root-cause analysis like the "5 Whys" technique.

Phase 3: **Design** involves brainstorming solutions, focusing on creating a Minimum Viable Product, developing rough prototypes, and using "Red Teaming" to proactively identify flaws.

Phase 4: **Deliver** is about launching the pilot with a clear message that it's a test for learning. You invite honest feedback for iteration, recognizing that "progress doesn't happen in a straight line."

PART IV Experiment

PART

IV

Experiment

10

The EX Blueprint

Letting Everyone See the Big Picture

That last chapter was long, because it took that much to cover the inner workings of the extremely powerful process known as the Double Diamond.

Now you get a short chapter, but an important one—we cover a tool you can use at the end of the Double Diamond process.

The Employee Experience Blueprint

As you know, the co-designing mindset can be used on pretty much any size project. If it's a smaller one, then when you're done with the Double Diamond, you may have everything you need to implement your work product.

But let's say that's not the case, because you took on a larger project that has many moving parts. You need a way to organize who will do what, and how those actions will improve the employee experience. What you need is the EX Blueprint.

In Chapter 9, we looked at journey mapping. That's invaluable for documenting the current experience. **The EX Blueprint is about designing the future experience,** based on everything you learned and agreed upon in the Double Diamond process.

As with the journey map, you don't need fancy software to create an EX Blueprint; a simple spreadsheet will do. Figure 10.1 is an example of what we might create for the tuition reimbursement project we discussed and used as the basis for the journey map in Chapter 9.

We don't expect you to be able to read the tiny print, but just take in the overall layout. Below the figure, we'll talk about each element. By the way, if you would like a full-size template, just go to EXDBook.com and type in "EX Blueprint." We'll send it to you.

An efficient way to create this document is to get your team together that worked on the Double Diamond. Now it's time to grab more sticky notes and fill in the matrix. It's another case where people may need a little time to think over the details; therefore, it may be preferable to avoid one marathon session and instead fill it in over the course of a few days.

What the Rows Mean

The first row is "What we learned from the current Employee Journey." If your project didn't involve employee journey mapping, then this row would be what you learned from discovery in general.

The second row is "Front Stage: What we want employees to see." By "stage" we're using a performance metaphor where the employees are on the stage in a performance, but use whatever language works best for you.

The third row is "Back Stage: What our team needs to do" to make the Front Stage happen.

Finally, the fourth row is "Behind the Scenes: Policies, Processes, & Systems."

What the Columns Mean

Each column is a phase of the employee experience as it relates to this project. Therefore, we have the following columns:

- Awareness
- Getting Acquainted with Online System
- Determining Reimbursement Eligibility
- Applying for Reimbursement
- Receiving Reimbursement

EX Blueprint: Tuition Reimbursement Project

	DIMENSION			
	What we learned from the current Employee Journey	Front Stage: What we want employees to see	Back Stage: What our team needs to do	Behind the Scenes: Policies, Processes & Systems
STAGE 1 **Awareness**	Many people were unaware of the benefit; and even if they knew about it, they couldn't find info	Email announcement; dedicated web page; expanded search results; video walkthrough; employee handbook entry	Write emails; build web page; train search system on more terms; create video; update handbook	No new ones needed
STAGE 2 **Getting Acquainted with Online System**	Poor handoff to external portal; unclear instructions; poor support experience	Seamless integration of external portal; user-tested instructions and thorough FAQ	List all questions in last 6 months, and organize them; then either answer in FAQ or change labels to make clearer; create video walkthrough	Work with vendor to change labeling to match our needs
STAGE 3 **Determining Reimbursement Eligibility**	Confusing nomenclature; very thin FAQ; calls to Support for basic questions indicating poor labeling	Plenty of tooltips (when hovering) and thorough FAQ to minimize confusion	Continuously add to FAQ until obvious questions to Support go away; change labeling if necessary	Monitor program rule changes so we can let users know proactively instead of find out the hard way
STAGE 4 **Applying for Reimbursement**	People need to re-enter info because it's not saved dynamically between sessions; general unawareness of next steps	All their work is saved; progress bar so they know where they are in the process; FAQ nearby that's focused on application questions	Add relevant FAQ to each step; monitor abandons and follow up with them	Look into dynamic saving so no inputted data is lost; create progress bars
STAGE 5 **Receiving Reimbursement**	Users unaware of next steps and status of their applications	After an application is successfully filled out, users should see a page to that effect, with next steps outlined. Also, they should get regular emails to indicate current status and that the application is not lost	Write language for "success" page when app is filled out; write emails for status updates	Create "success" page with "what to expect" language; set up email sequence with periodic status updates

Figure 10.1 The EX Blueprint.

Now it's time to fill out the matrix, first with what we know about each stage and then what we're going to implement.

Stage 1 Column: Awareness

What we learned: Many people were unaware of the benefit; and even if they knew about it, they couldn't find info

What we want employees to see: Email announcement; dedicated web page; expanded search results; video walkthrough; employee handbook entry

What our team needs to do: Write emails; build web page; train search system on more terms; create video; update handbook

Policies, Processes & Systems: No new ones needed

Stage 2 Column: Getting Acquainted with Online System

What we learned: Poor handoff to external portal; unclear instructions; poor support experience

What we want employees to see: Seamless integration of external portal; user-tested instructions and thorough FAQ

What our team needs to do: List all questions in last six months and organize them; then either answer in FAQ or change labels to make clearer; create video walkthrough

Policies, Processes & Systems: Work with vendor to change labeling to match our needs

Stage 3 Column: Determining Reimbursement Eligibility

What we learned: Confusing labeling; very thin FAQ; calls to Support for basic questions indicating poor labeling

What we want employees to see: Plenty of tooltips (when hovering) and thorough FAQ to minimize confusion

What our team needs to do: Continuously add to FAQ until obvious questions to Support go away; change labeling if necessary

Policies, Processes & Systems: Monitor program rule changes so we can let users know proactively instead of finding out the hard way

Stage 4 Column: Applying for Reimbursement

What we learned: People need to re-enter info because it's not saved dynamically between sessions; general unawareness of next steps

What we want employees to see: All their work is saved; progress bar so they know where they are in the process; FAQ nearby that's focused on application questions

What our team needs to do: Add relevant FAQ to each step; monitor abandons and follow up with them

Policies, Processes & Systems: Look into dynamic saving so no inputted data is lost; create progress bars

Stage 5 Column: Receiving Reimbursement

What we learned: Users unaware of next steps and status of their applications

What we want employees to see: After an application is successfully filled out, users should see a page to that effect, with next steps outlined. Also, they should get regular emails to indicate current status and that the application is not lost

What our team needs to do: Write language for "success" page when app is filled out; write emails for status updates

Policies, Processes & Systems: Create "success" page with "what to expect" language; set up email sequence with periodic status updates

The beauty of the EX Blueprint is how well it provides a succinct overview on one page. Leaders and anyone else can look at the blueprint and see the big picture: What we learned during discovery, what we'll implement, and how it involves various stakeholders.

By now, you can probably predict what we're going to say next: This is a living document. You want people to read it and suggest improvements, which they'll surely have once they can see the big picture that the blueprint provides.

Notice also how you'll be making life easier for busy leaders: No fat binders to review, but a one-page overview that covers the bases. It's another design element that people appreciate.

In this chapter, we covered another highly effective tool that you may choose to augment the Double Diamond process. Because this is a

> *Leaders and anyone else can look at the blueprint and see the big picture: What we learned during discovery, what we'll implement, and how it involves various stakeholders.*

handbook and not an encyclopedia, we've not covered all the tools that practitioners use to do EX Design. Please keep in mind that you can make a great deal of progress in your organization with just the tools and methods we've discussed.

In fact, we'll go one step further and encourage you to implement what we've covered before you look for further tools. We mentioned the Silicon Valley saying: "You don't learn until you ship." The same is true here: When you "ship" your first co-created project, you'll be in a much better position to know what other tools and aids you could use. At that point, please contact us at the address in the back of this book and we'd be happy to recommend other resources, based on your needs.

Chapter Summary

The EX Blueprint is a tool for the end of the Double Diamond process, used to design the future experience based on learnings.

The Blueprint is structured as a matrix with rows representing insights from the current employee journey ("What we learned"), desired employee experience ("Front Stage"), team actions ("Back Stage"), and underlying policies/processes/systems ("Behind the Scenes").

Columns in the Blueprint represent different stages of the employee experience related to the project (for example, Awareness, Getting Acquainted with Online System, etc.).

The Blueprint provides a succinct, one-page overview for stakeholders, making it easier for leaders to understand the big picture and facilitating continuous iteration.

11 | A Conversation with Melanie Rosenwasser

Bringing UX Rigor to EX: It's a Product, Not a Perk

Background

Mel and I (Samantha) were introduced by our mutual friend, Brian Elliott, who thought we'd hit it off, and he was absolutely right. From our first conversation, we connected over our shared belief that HR can and should adopt product- and design-led ways of working.

What I found so energizing about Mel is how she didn't just talk about the shift—she made it happen. Her story of retraining her entire team and embedding new practices into the Dropbox Virtual First operating model is an incredible example of what's possible when leaders commit to change. We've loved learning from each other, and I'm so excited for you to hear her story; it's full of practical insight and big inspiration.

Could you please tell us a little about your background and how you landed where you are?

I have a degree in finance, and I spent about five years in corporate finance before moving into HR. I've held a number of HR roles in compensation, learning and development, and HR business partnering at companies like GE and Apple, prior to coming to Dropbox. Today I'm the Chief People Officer at Dropbox. I've been here for 10 years.

How did you make the jump from finance to HR? What made you want to do that?

Great question. I was in a rotational development program at Gillette, the razor blade company in Boston. It was an incredibly difficult program to get into. They had thousands of applications and only hired three of us, so it was a really big opportunity for me.

On the second day there, I was staring at a spreadsheet, and I thought, *I hate this.* Part of my job later was to go to a number of career fairs at universities to help recruit the next class of folks coming to the development program.

At the fairs, I was like, "Wow, I've never been a part of this. Is this a job that people work full time?" My friend said: "Yeah. It's called recruiting." I said: "What's recruiting?" That's how I became interested in HR. To me it was the intersection of people and business, and it gave me a lot of energy.

The problem was that the program didn't allow me to simply switch to HR, so I finished that three-year program. I then ended up getting a job in compensation as my first role in HR, because it's the most closely connected to finance in terms of skill sets.

Early in my career, I thought I had lost so much time being in the wrong discipline of finance. But having analytical capability at the time I was coming up through HR, it was the only differentiating skill set I had. In hindsight, I'm so grateful for the time I spent there. Especially now: Everything's about ROI and success metrics—tying business outcomes to the work that we do.

How did you get interested in EX in the first place?

I started to realize how much the HR funnel resembled the product funnel. If you compare the product funnel to HR: The top of the product funnel is awareness and for HR it's talent brand campaigns. Then for products it's acquisition, which for HR is sourcing and recruiting. With products it's conversion, and in HR it's when candidates accept offers. Products have customer retention and HR has employee engagement and now also employee experience. That is the phase where we spend the bulk of our time in HR. Products have advocacy, and our equivalent is employee referrals. Finally, customers churn out of products and when employees churn out of our organization, they become alumni.

I've come to talk about Employee Experience as a set of products, because that is essentially speaking the same language as my peers and colleagues at Dropbox. I work alongside some of the best product managers and designers in the industry. They love the idea of applying their craft more broadly and have been really helpful in our journey of bringing this concept of "HR as a Product" to life at Dropbox.

> *I've come to talk about Employee Experience as a set of products, because that is essentially speaking the same language as my peers and colleagues at Dropbox.*

Can you tell us a little about how you apply EX at Dropbox—what works and what hasn't?

You and I have different names for the same thing: When you refer to Employee Experience Design, I've found it useful to call it "HR as a Product." To me that refers to a cohesive set of products across our People team, like performance management, learning, and comp, where employees and candidates are our customers.

To bring this concept to life, I wanted to come up with a framework that made sense for our team. We researched and analyzed different product management and design best practices and frameworks: Design Thinking; the Lean Startup Model; the Double Diamond Model; and others. We then took all of these and created a tailored approach that aligns with our unique needs.

We ended up with a four-step framework. The steps are: Discover, Build, Evaluate, Iterate. If you look at the other models I mentioned, they all follow a similar pattern, but this one works for our needs as an HR organization.

Discover for us is truly understanding the customer problem. **Build** is about creating prototypes or minimum viable products and testing them. **Evaluate** is about analyzing outcomes against success metrics, which could be adoption, engagement, or attrition. Finally, **Iterate** is more about incorporating that feedback, debugging the product, and eventually scaling.

I realize there's a huge change-management component to migrating an entire HR team to this way of thinking. I've thought about this in terms of mindset shifts:

- Human Centered: from HR Driven to Employee Driven
- Simple is Sophisticated: from Fragmented Complexity to Intuitive Simplicity
- Stay Curious: from Defensiveness to Openness
- Outcomes over Outputs: from Task Creation to Value Creation
- Iterate to Innovate: from Perfection Seeking to Progress Making

I know that's covering a lot of ground, but let's just look at the "Stay Curious" one: Traditional HR practitioners are not programmed to be comfortable with constant constructive criticism. You're usually trying to get something to roughly 95 percent perfect before you ship it. That's the opposite of what we're trying to go for here.

Didn't you have something called Virtual First where you used your framework to address the whole office/remote experience?

Yes. Virtual First is Dropbox's working model that combines remote work flexibility with intentional in-person connection. It's not fully remote, it's not hybrid, and it's not traditional office based. It's effectively its own category.

It's where remote work is the primary experience for all of our employees, but we gather quarterly with our teams for strategic alignment, innovation, and bonding. We think it's the best of all worlds. Keep in mind that prior to the pandemic, Dropbox was 97 percent in-office, and we had invested a ton in the in-office experience. So, the transition to Virtual First represented a total overhaul of not just where we work, but how we work.

We evolved the Employee Value Proposition from in-office entitlements like gyms and free food to flexibility. And we built this entire category based on product and design principles.

In the Discover phase, we did a lot of focus groups and surveys, plus research on internal trends and stats on performance and productivity. We interviewed dozens of companies, including hybrid and completely remote tech companies.

We learned something interesting about hybrid arrangements. When you have some employees that choose to go into the office and some that choose to work from home, you end up with uneven performance outcomes and uneven promotion outcomes: I'm going into the office every day and my manager is in the office every day. I'm getting more face time with that manager, and that can create an uneven playing field.

We also found that when we surveyed employees about how they wanted to work, there was no consensus. Some wanted to go back to the office, some wanted completely remote, and some wanted hybrid. What we ultimately gleaned was that although they weren't aligned on a specific way of working, they were aligned on the notion of choice.

> *Although they weren't aligned on a specific way of working, they were aligned on the notion of choice.*

The value of flexibility and autonomy. Our design brief became: "How do we design a way of working that enables flexibility and autonomy, while addressing the known challenges of distributed work?"

When we moved to the Build phase, we developed certain principles:

1. Individual work is always done at home. There is no desk hoteling and no hybrid, so you're avoiding some of those hybrid drawbacks.
2. On Zoom, everyone has their own tile. If you happen to be in the office for a meeting, you'll still be in your own Zoom tile. It's a great equalizer.
3. We created this practice called Async by Default. What this means is we do a lot of context sharing and even decision-making asynchronously. (Note: This is an IT term that refers to doing work non-simultaneously, and instead when it works for you.)
4. We put into place something called core collaboration hours, which are overlapping meeting windows. So, on the West Coast they are 9 a.m. to 1 p.m. which matches with people on the East Coast whose meeting window is noon to 4 p.m. The rest of your workday is your time for work, designed however works best for you. We knew that just moving the previous in-office practices to a remote context was broken—eight straight hours of meetings in an office didn't work. So why would that work for you on Zoom?

5. We transformed our traditional offices into Dropbox Studios. These reimagined spaces encourage collaboration and community-building by giving employees different options for collaboration including casual gathering spaces for conversation, coworking areas, conference rooms, and classrooms for organized group learning.
6. We revised our perks program. Previously in the office, you got many amazing perks. Now we have all of that in the form of an allowance, so you choose what's important to you: It could be used for childcare, a gym membership, or expanding your home office setup.
7. We also have Dropbox Neighborhoods, where employees who are in or around the same city can come together for events, even if they're not on the same team.
8. We do quarterly team gatherings, as I mentioned. But we have an Offsite Planning Team that helps to put together your event. If you're an accounting manager, you're probably not also an experienced event planner, and planning really intentional gatherings can take a lot of time and effort.
9. We open-source all of our learnings and share them. We've created a Virtual First Toolkit, where we've designed a variety of frameworks and tools on topics like team effectiveness and communicating in a remote environment.

How did you come up with those principles like Async by Default?

It was through a lot of our focus group work, asking things like: "What's broken about your workday?" and then we tried to design around it. In some cases, we designed our own solution; in others, we adopted practices from other companies where we knew they worked. Why reinvent the wheel?

The idea of Async by Default is something that GitLab uses. They are an all-remote company, and they've been all remote from day one. They write everything down and publish it to the world so you can actually see how they run their company, completely remotely. It's impressive. Their management process is completely transparent.

We just talked about the Discover and Build phases. The next phase is Evaluate. Given that we rolled out Virtual First during the pandemic, it's hard not to conflate negative employee sentiment with Virtual First.

That's because when we rolled it out, we were virtual only: We couldn't show employees the magic of gathering, which is part of our vision. So, we had a rocky start with respect to sentiment.

Once we were out of the pandemic, we could finally show folks that we cared deeply about in-person connection and the neighborhood events. We then saw the highest employee engagement scores that we've ever had.

We also saw record-low attrition rates. They decreased by 20 percent when we went Virtual First. We improved all of our hiring metrics: This past year we had the highest offer acceptance rates in the history of the company, and the lowest time to close. More than 70 percent of our candidates say Virtual First is the reason they're even interested in talking to us. When we survey our employees internally, 90 percent of them attribute their retention to the flexibility they get from Virtual First.

> More than 70 percent of our candidates say Virtual First is the reason they're even interested in talking to us. When we survey our employees internally, 90 percent of them attribute their retention to the flexibility they get from Virtual First.

As you know, a lot of companies are mandating a return to office and they're saying, "it's for culture" or "it's for collaboration." Well, Dropbox was actually voted the number one tech company for culture and values in 2023, and we're fully remote. We've enjoyed seeing this kind of progress.

Finally, we have the Iterate phase. It's not perfect, and there's a tax you pay as a remote company. For example, we found that when people were gathering, they were doing so with their immediate team, so they missed out on the opportunity to bond with cross-functional colleagues. In response, we created a company-wide offsite calendar so leaders could see what offsites are being planned around the globe, across every team and function. Now, if you want to plan your offsite to overlap with a cross-functional team, you can.

We also found that working from home facilitates a lot of sedentary work. We therefore created a "Meet and Move" pilot. If you joined the pilot, it meant you went for a walk and took your meeting on the phone instead of sitting on Zoom. We saw a 30 percent lift in energy levels post meeting, just from that pilot.

Did everybody in a meeting need to be on a walk, or was it just if you wanted to?

People would opt into the pilot and any meetings that they had during this pilot phase, they would not take sitting down at their computer. So, it was fine if you wanted to go for a walk in your neighborhood or walk around your house or to a coffee shop. Just anything that was not sitting at your desk where you normally work.

As a final example, when we created the neighborhood events, we thought attendance would be high for things like happy hours and social gatherings. It turns out that employees actually wanted a reason to gather that was tied to the company mission. So, we reimagined these events around a purpose. It might be a company all-hands meeting, a product release, or a fireside chat with execs who happened to be in that city.

With all these examples, we found that we were pressure-testing our hypotheses constantly. We're still learning every day, and we share with employees not only the things that work well, but also the things that go poorly.

Was there much resistance to using your framework the way you did?

We needed to gain buy-in from the executive team on the new value proposition and the idea that when employees have better experiences, their productivity increases, and so does their engagement and retention.

Of course, there was a cost-savings element, because you're no longer tethered to these long-term commercial leases. But we're not just putting that money back into our pockets. Instead of paying rent for offices, we've invested in on-demand spaces, where employees can use an app to book a space to work, essentially in any city in the world. We also invest heavily in employee training. For example, we offer training on things ranging from AI to best practices in communication—like clear and direct writing—which is crucial in a remote-first world. We believe companies need to invest in these new ways of working.

We noticed other benefits. For example, the culture has changed dramatically because we have diversified our employee base. Now we can recruit from everywhere. Previously, we were drawing mainly from tech companies and tech schools. What you get then is a lot of sameness; all the tech companies are fishing in the same pond. Now that we've been able to hire from anywhere, we have a diversity of experience that's really working for us. The workforce is more resilient because many come from industries outside of just tech.

Going back to when you had to influence execs in order to get this across the line, what got them there? Was it the cost savings or was it they believed that employee experience would create better business outcomes?

I think it was the latter. It was the excitement around pioneering a new work environment. It also went hand-in-hand with our products. Dropbox is a product that connects distributed teams, so what better way to build for distributed teams than to actually be one? We are building for ourselves every day. The mission and the employee experience have merged into one.

Our execs were also convinced by the amount of research we did. We had a great deal of performance data pre- and post-remote work. We could show through data how the previously held notions of "You must be in person to be productive" and "You must be in person to have a great culture" were not true.

We could show through data how the previously held notions of "You must be in person to be productive" and "You must be in person to have a great culture" were not true.

Some people say that companies that sell products have an easier time doing EXD than other types of organizations. What's your opinion on that?

I don't think employee experience necessarily means distributed work or technology companies. It's a way of building and iterating on an experience. It's not just for HR, and it's not just for employees. These principles can just as easily apply to a finance team. If you're a finance team, you have the same customers that HR has. There are a lot of interactions that people will have with a finance team every single day. How do you create those touch points so they're seamless, positive experiences?

Did you find anybody in the leadership ranks or elsewhere, where they never came around? They decided that Virtual First wasn't for them and left?

Our senior leadership team clearly understood our vision with Virtual First, but we did have some employees who chose to opt out.

They said: "I'm never going to adopt core collaboration hours. I don't believe this is going to help us." They didn't leave because of it, but they were not necessarily subscribing to what we were selling.

In practice is where we saw a shift in some of our employees, like a major life event or change. For example, one of our VPs—who was a naysayer—went on maternity leave and came back to work. She said, "This is the best thing that has ever happened to me in my professional life. Now, when I wake up in the morning, I'm not sending my child to daycare and getting in my car to commute for 90 minutes. I have that time with her. I can spend the morning with my child, and that's an opportunity I never would have had if I didn't have this flexibility."

The beautiful thing about employee experience is people opt in and opt out, and over time you will have more people opting in for that experience than those who are not interested and leave. Because of that, you're going to see a lift in some things like retention and engagement.

What do you feel are the most important aspects of employee experience design?

If I had to pick a specific area, it's probably the importance of feedback and iteration. With products and beta testing, more users equals more feedback, which equals more opportunities for improvement. It's the same with employee experience. You leverage pilots to truly pressure test what you came up with and whether it drives the outcome you want.

You leverage pilots to truly pressure test what you came up with and whether it drives the outcome you want.

When you started the EXD journey, did you find that maybe people weren't as open early on as they are now, because they weren't sure if they could be honest?

We have a lot of touch points in terms of employee listening. We do biannual employee engagement surveys, and our CEO reads every single comment. They are anonymized and because of that, people are very honest. We also do tons of focus groups, deep dives, and pilots with employees. Through this, they know we're building together.

The decision to go Virtual First was not necessarily employee driven. But once we made that decision, we were building with employees around how we were going to make this work. Because they became part of the design, and they got to give their input, their engagement increased.

The culture of our company is one where nobody is afraid to tell you what they really think. We had a lot of built-in touch points, but building alongside and building together was also especially helpful.

What are some common misunderstandings or myths that you think people have about EXD?

That it takes too long, or it's too complex. It may also seem very technical, but it's actually not. It's just a way of thinking through something that we've been doing for a really long time. I also think a lot of practitioners are doing this, but they're doing it in pieces, or for a specific program. It's about getting folks to understand these are things you're already doing, and here's how you could do them better or more often.

Let's say you were introduced to an organization that's new to you. How would you assess where they are on the EXD spectrum from terrible to amazing?

I would ask them a set of questions.

1. How are your company values reflected in the day to day?
2. How personalized is the employee journey, from recruitment all the way through offboarding?
3. What formal listening mechanisms do you have in place: Are there surveys? Polls? Focus groups? All of the above?
4. How is that feedback actually translated into action?
5. How sophisticated is your People Analytics function? That's very important because so much of this work is being able to measure outcomes so that you at least have a starting point. You need to know whether or not you're improving. You've got to have data integrity.
6. Finally, how has senior leadership communicated and demonstrated their commitment to employee experience?

You asked: "How sophisticated is your People Analytics function?" If somebody said it's "reasonably sophisticated," how would you dig in there? What sort of litmus test would you have for them?

It's about how you measure success across all of your people functions. In recruiting, there's a set of metrics that are table stakes, like offer acceptance rates. But there's a higher level of sophistication around measuring your quality of hire. It's the same with learning and development: A basic answer would be: "We measured attendance, and then we asked people if they'll apply their learnings." That's table stakes. An advanced way of measuring L&D is we measured the starting competency about something, and it was X. Then after the course, it was Y. You're actually measuring competency. You can also measure the promotion rate for people who have gone through this training versus people who haven't, and you look for a difference.

If you came across an organization that really needed some help, where would you start? What would be the first action that you'd recommend?

The simplest way is to define the employee problems you and your team are passionate about solving. Then describe the top three in the form of problem statements.

Define the employee problems you and your team are passionate about solving. Then describe the top three in the form of problem statements.

That's where I would start. Then you need to gather information for your first pressure test: Are these really the top three problems? Then create a pilot with a Minimum Viable Product. Figure out how you will measure success, and iterate.

Knowing what you know now about employee experience design and thinking about the organizations you have been part of, what would you do differently if you had a second chance?

I would have started earlier. I've been at Dropbox for 10 years and was at Apple previously. These are user-centered technology companies, and I could have been speaking the same language as my CEO and my colleagues, except about employees.

Looking back, what were you thinking at the time that initially took you in a different direction from traditional approaches to addressing employee experience?

It's not that I dismissed it but more that I had to discover it. I started hearing about "productization of HR." But earlier in my career, it was more like, "Melanie, our performance management isn't working. What are we going to do about it?" And instead of deciding to think about this as a product issue, I was really more just hair-on-fire reactive.

Now that I've been in the role for a while, I can take a step back and say: "OK, we're meeting the baseline needs, so how do we up our game?" Early on, I think it may have been too hard for me when I was still learning the ropes of this job and just trying to get the tactics across the finish line to truly step back and think about it in this way.

Do you think in order to take an EX approach, you first need an HR foundation?

The earlier you can introduce people to these concepts, the better. I teach at the Human Capital Management Master's Program at Columbia. One of the classes I teach has a section about applying design thinking to employee experience. I see this as a huge win because we're seeding this concept with students who are studying HR.

I emphasize to them that if you go into an interview and you say, "My philosophy is around applying design thinking to employee experience," you will have a leg up over everybody else who's interviewing.

The earlier people get experience with this, the better. I do simulations and case studies with them in class: "Here's a problem statement. Use the design-thinking methodology to map out how you might attack this." It's about getting your brain to think this way early on.

What about some people who may think: *EXD is giving away my power. I worked for this. I worked to be in the position of making policy, not sharing it.*

It depends on the project. There are certain things that are ripe for employee experience or design thinking and things that aren't, like compliance. The head of compliance might reasonably believe that's not something we're going to crowdsource. But performance management is, and so is compensation planning. Many things that touch both employees and managers would benefit. For the areas that don't lend themselves to co-design, that's OK. You don't have to do those things, and can pick other ones that you think are the most critical.

HR professionals have spent a long time building their value around their expertise and experience. Are you saying that besides expertise and experience, there are other ways of approaching this?

We have a Slack channel for new products that we are building, and we dog food all of them with our employees. We say if you have feedback on this new product, go to this Slack channel and give us your opinion. There are hundreds of pieces of feedback like: "This doesn't work ... Why did you decide to do it this way? ... This button doesn't make sense."

And the product managers say, "Thank you! Awesome!" They too are experts at what they do, but they're not offended at all. They are so grateful because they know if they can address even 50 percent of what these folks are saying, their product is going to be 10 times better before it reaches the next group of users.

> *It's a different way of thinking. Being really upfront about what doesn't work—and inviting people to poke holes—makes whatever I'm delivering 10 times better.*

It's a different way of thinking. Being really upfront about what doesn't work—and inviting people to poke holes—makes whatever I'm delivering 10 times better. It's changing your thinking a little bit to be like a product manager, except for people.

Thank you so much for your thoughts and insights, Melanie!
You're very welcome.

Chapter Summary

Melanie describes applying EX at Dropbox as "HR as a Product," aligning HR processes with product management and design best practices, and viewing employees and candidates as customers.

Dropbox developed a four-step framework: Discover, Build, Evaluate, and Iterate.

Melanie highlights key mindset shifts required for an HR team to embrace this approach, such as moving from "HR Driven to Employee Driven" and "Perfection Seeking to Progress Making."

She shares the case study of Dropbox's "Virtual First" operating model, detailing how it was designed and iterated through the four-step framework, resulting in higher engagement and record-low attrition.

Melanie emphasizes that EX principles are broadly applicable beyond HR or tech companies and stresses the importance of feedback and iteration as the most crucial aspects of EXD.

PART V
Measure

12 | Metrics That Matter

Taking the Pulse of Your Organization

We've already discussed how some people will rush into a project and not follow the discipline of the Double Diamond for two reasons—because they're unaware of it, or because they're busy and want to get to a quick result.

The same thing happens with metrics. It's common to hear:

- "Too much analysis paralysis ... let's get on with it!"
- "I've been in this business a very long time and trust me—I know what success looks like."
- "The only metrics that really matter are money in the bank and share price."

Those are all excuses for not measuring. The only thing worse is measuring progress using the typical annual engagement survey. Why is it worse? Because it's usually done so poorly that it yields no useful information, but the act of doing it gives people a false sense of accomplishment. In Chapter 2, we described how annual surveys are a snapshot in time, but organizations change by the day. That's just one of the problems with them.

In a moment, you'll get a list you can use to think through and gauge the quality of any survey you do—or any measurements you take, for that matter. In fact, the insights in this chapter by themselves can be transformative to your organization—if you choose to take action on them.

Before we go any deeper, let's clear up the difference between metrics and measurements. A metric is the dimension we want to focus on, and a measurement is a data point. Temperature is the metric or dimension, and 98 degrees is the measurement. Another metric is YTD Offer-Acceptance Rate, and the raw measurement might be that today we received acceptances for five job offers. We can then collect that granular data, along with the number of offers made, to enable us to calculate the metric.

GPS Navigation for EX Projects

Let's think for a moment about the experience of traveling in a car before we had GPS. The old-school car dashboard told you how fast you were going. That's helpful, but what if you're going 75 mph in the wrong direction?

Now, when you settle behind the wheel and have GPS, you're in better hands: It will tell you how fast you're going, if you're headed in the right direction, and much more, as long as you meet one condition: You must answer when it asks: "Where do you want to go?"

If you don't get the destination part right, the rest won't matter.

If you don't get the destination part right, the rest won't matter, regardless of how expensive your sports car is, or how great of a driver you are.

We discussed in Chapter 3 how EX initiatives need to be aligned with organizational outcomes in order to be the most effective, and the same is true with your metrics. They need to meet two tests:

1. Are you choosing metrics that are **capable of telling you** if you're delivering on the employee experience?
2. Once you choose them, are you designing the metrics so they're **administered properly**?

This distinction can be a little confusing, so here's another analogy: Let's say someone is concerned about their liver. The doctor may say that a blood test is in order, and not some other test like an ultrasound. Then the challenge becomes administering the test correctly. It may be the right test, but maybe the person eats too much before the test, the sample gets contaminated, or too much time goes by before the sample is analyzed. They need the right test administered in the right way in order to get useful information.

They need the right test administered in the right way in order to get useful information.

In our experience, all organizations have at least a few metrics, but few are methodical about choosing the right ones, and then implementing them to deliver maximum value.

Using questions to build a solid foundation

Everyone is familiar with what you might call "questions for understanding." Those can range from "How's work going?" to highly specific questions in a survey. What's less common are questions for planning, but they're vital to ask, think about, and answer, in order to set your metrics up for success. We've already covered some of these in earlier chapters, but let's look at the entire sequence of questions for planning:

1. **How do we determine what the issue is that we want to focus on?** We discussed this in Chapter 9 and will come back to it in Chapter 15.
2. **What is the extent of the issue?** As you know, the Know Think Suspect workshop is one way to determine this. Other methods are surveys, focus groups, individual conversations, and so on.
3. **What is our goal?** If you created a problem statement, which we also discussed in Chapter 9, then you will have reached some consensus in your team about what exactly is our goal or benefit if we fix the problem.
4. **How will we know when we've achieved our goal?** This is also part of a good problem statement. It makes us avoid generalities like "significantly improve" and get to something we can measure.
5. **Which tools should we use now and later to measure our progress?** For example, Kirsty Lloyd mentioned in Chapter 6 about Haka House that they started with Know Think Suspect workshops, did subsequent interviews, and later followed up with surveys.

Considerations for getting useful information

If you've followed the five questions above, that means you've indeed created a solid foundation and are ready to gather the data you need. You've **matched the right tools for your project.** Now let's talk about how to make sure you use the tools in a way that gives you **valid insights.**

1. **Do we rely only on a survey?** A well-structured survey is a fine way to gather some of what you need, but the operative word is *some*. A survey doesn't give you the back-and-forth that a conversation is so useful for. A focus group allows for piggybacking on ideas that even a great survey cannot do. With so many ways to gather information, don't limit yourself to just one method. If you contact us at the web address at the back of this handbook, we can send you a "Which Tool When" chart that's a good reference.

2. **Does a metric capture what matters?** Here's an example of a question we've actually seen used: "Do you have a great leader at work?" (And it was asked only once a year.) Is that referring to my manager, or might it mean the CEO? Also, I've had two managers in the last few months; do they mean over the last year or some other period? And what exactly does "great" mean? Someone who checks all the boxes? Or the best I've had in my career?

   Is it capturing what managers value, or is it measuring what employees want? Or maybe what the board wants?

   There's also a big-picture consideration about your metric: Is it capturing what managers value, or is it measuring what employees want? Or maybe what the board wants? It could be that employees at a certain organization want clear instructions, but managers want people who take the initiative and figure things out on their own. And what if the board has pushed for aggressive cost-cutting measures: How they define a well-run organization might be the opposite of what employees have in mind.

3. **Do we establish baselines and measure against them?** If you have a question that asks people to rate something on a scale of 1–10 and you get a result of 5.5, is that good? Maybe that's the highest ever

recorded—or the lowest. And maybe the overall score has held steady for the organization as a whole, but there have been wild swings in different departments. It's crucial that you're clear on what you will compare the results against. And when you get data for the first time on a particular metric, be sure to let people know not to jump to conclusions about what it means until you've had a chance to establish a solid baseline. More on this in a minute.

4. **Do we make it safe to give honest feedback?** Some organizations have a culture where people speak their minds, and other organizations are the opposite, where you soon learn the perils of being honest. If you want to cultivate an atmosphere where constructive criticism is welcome, then you have two tasks: First to say so clearly, and second, to show by your actions that you mean it. In the interview with Greg Pryor in the next chapter, you will see how the tone at one well-known company was set from the top.

Another way to get people to speak their minds is to be clear how the information will be handled. Most people know that online surveys can be identified down to the user, so how are we putting people's minds to rest that their opinions will be confidential? When a department head directly asked Kirsty in Chapter 6 to give him the complete records of her conversations with his staff, she said that was not going to happen.

When you report results, it's good policy to have a minimum response threshold of some number like five or ten. In other words, report the results at a department level only for departments that have at least five employees, or for demographics of at least five people. For example, maybe we just hired two people to be our "AI Department" or we only have three people in the company who come from the Pacific Islands. Because those numbers are below our threshold of, say, five, then we'll never display separate results of that department or demographic. Their numbers will be aggregated with other units.

It may be that you need to go through a few cycles of reporting before people actually believe that it's safe to be honest, depending on the history of that organization. It's also a good idea to be explicit about the policy on a regular basis, because new hires bring their assortment of past experiences with them.

5. **Do we review questions for bias?** Our earlier example of a terrible question was: "Do you have a great leader at work?" That's also a biased way of phrasing the question. It's not hard to imagine a very different result if the question were phrased in the opposite way: "Do you have a poor leader at work?"

This kind of bias is incredibly common, partly because we're exposed to it from a young age. Simple statements like: "Wasn't that fun?" or "Do you like the present you just got?" get the message across very quickly, even to preschooler brains, that the answer should be "yes" because you're supposed to like it.

Twenty thousand questions later, when we're in the workforce, we don't bat an eye when we read survey questions like: "How easy was this product to use?" and "Our previous feedback survey showed that most people like our transportation-voucher benefit. Do you agree?" A quick review of your most-recent surveys should reveal whether this type of bias is an issue in your organization.

6. **Do we ask questions as frequently as is effective?** We already mentioned how the annual survey is about as useful as an annual temperature reading. If you have done your homework and identified certain drivers of employee engagement and satisfaction, then there is some urgency to establish a baseline and then measure how your efforts are being received.

If you ask too frequently about something—and if employees see no progress being made—you'll create question fatigue.

It's also important not to overdo it. If you ask too frequently about something—and if employees see no progress being made—you'll create question fatigue. In the next chapter, you'll hear about a good way to avoid this situation.

7. **Do we get as granular as practical?** Generally speaking, averages are a terrible way to report results. An exception would be as we mentioned in #4 above, where you want to maintain confidentiality among small numbers of respondents. Otherwise, averages can easily mask what's really going on.

Take a survey that asks for ratings on a scale as follows:

1 = terrible; 2 = poor; 3 = fair; 4 = good; and 5 = excellent. Let's say we asked four questions, and we reported back that we're not doing too badly! We got an average of 3, which is "fair"—you know, middle of the road.

The problem is if we reported the granular results, they'd show that we scored "poor" on two questions and "good" on two other questions. An organization making any effort at EX will want alarm bells going off for the "poor" ratings. The insights are not in the averages; they're in the signals you see only when you drill into the numbers.

> *The insights are not in the averages; they're in the signals you see only when you drill into the numbers.*

8. **Do we wait for statistical significance?** In school, we learn lots of things that we don't really need to remember later, like the Smoot-Hawley Act, or how to dissect a frog. Statistics are different: It's useful to learn—and then remember and use your whole life—the concept of statistical significance.

If you skipped that lecture in school, statistical significance is all about separating the signal from the noise—the important change, if there is one, versus just random results. People are constantly tempted to jump to conclusions when reviewing results, saying things like: "Ah hah! I was right!," or "Just give me the results as they start to come in." Human DNA seems to be built to use our eyes—or the seat of our pants—when judging success or failure, and to not wait *until the math tells us what we're looking at*. But that's what we need to do.

It's common for results to swing wildly at first, before they settle down . . . and . . . finally . . . reach a point where you can call a winner, loser, or inconclusive. Only occasionally will you have a winner right out of the gate that stays a winner the whole time.

Waiting for statistical significance is vital, because if you prematurely draw conclusions from data that should keep on being collected, then you risk changing direction when you shouldn't have or keeping on course when you shouldn't have.

If you need a refresher on these statistics, just consult your favorite AI tool. It may also give you tips about how to get others to hang on until the results are in.

9. **Do we promptly act on what we learn?** When employees take the time to respond to surveys, participate in focus groups, and so on, they're making an investment of their time and thoughts. They then wait to see if that investment pays off. If nothing comes of it, they rightly conclude that they wasted their time, and many will not bother again.

We don't always move ahead in a straight line, but the point is we're moving and we are trying.

We may have reasons for not yet reporting: "But what if the survey results were inconclusive? What if the new vacation policy we were so enthusiastic about was a dud?" Then say so. Be up front about what happened, and reinforce the point that we're in this together and we're testing different solutions. We don't always move ahead in a straight line, but the point is we're moving and we are trying. With that kind of message, people will see that their investment has paid off in being part of the rare organization that communicates well, tries stuff, and wants our help to find improvements.

Seven of our favorite questions

Sometimes the simplest questions can be among the most thought-provoking and valuable. We have seven favorite ones that work especially well when you're speaking individually with people, but they can also work in groups and even when delivered by survey. They are:

1. Why did you join?
2. Why do you stay?
3. What do you love?
4. Why would you leave?
5. What's getting in your way?

6. Would you agree or disagree with the following statement: "For what I put into my work, I believe the organization gives back equal or greater value to my life." (More on this in Chapter 15.)
7. Read on for the seventh question, because it takes some explanation.

They're straightforward, and they cover so much of the employee experience.

A most unusual question that can deliver extraordinary insights

I (Dean) want to tell you about the time I and a couple of my associates hit some pay dirt that turned into an absolute gold mine.

At the time, I was CHRO at Sears. We had 270,000 employees, and it was a really stressful period. This was when Sears—which had been the dominant retailer in America and possibly the world—was being challenged by the likes of Amazon. Needless to say, I had a tight budget and a massive organization to stay on top of.

So you have a bit of background, I had interviewed with Eddie Lampert, the owner of Sears. When Eddie offered me the job, he took a book and slid it across the table to me. He said: "I need data. Talk to me with data." The book was called: *Analytics at Work* by Tom Davenport.[1] I had my marching orders.

To be honest, some of what we were doing at Sears was not in the category of proactive EX design, but looked more like putting out fires. When we got to work each morning, we knew we'd be dealing with every kind of HR issue, but it was all so reactive. How could we get ahead of the problems by having a leading indicator that things were about to blow up, instead of a lagging indicator of how large the explosion was?

We decided to hack the time-clock system. In case you don't know about "punching in" and "punching out," it goes back to the industrial age when workers would file by a special clock that punched their time card as they arrived and left. We had a form of that at Sears, so it was a moment of the day that almost all employees shared.

---

[1] Davenport, Thomas H., Jeanne G. Harris, and Robert Morison. *Analytics at Work: Smarter Decisions, Better Results.* Boston, MA: Harvard Business Press, 2010.

Our hack to the system was to ask you to choose an emoji for your energy level as you punched your time card, answering the question: "How are you feeling right now?" This was actually before emojis were a thing; we called it "mood ring." You could choose from five faces, ranging from exhausted to full of energy. We ran two pilots—one that asked the question in the morning, and one when you checked out—and discovered through testing that it was best to ask this question at the end of the day.

At this point, you may be thinking: Didn't people just tell you what they thought you wanted to hear? The answer is yes—for a few days. We measured that too, and on average it took five days to get to the truth. We'd see: "Full of Energy! ... Full of Energy! ... Full of Energy! ... Full of Energy! ... Okay ... Exhausted!..." We needed those five responses to begin to get meaningful information.

> *Every day, we were receiving 70 thousand data points.*

When we turned this system on, we got a Niagara Falls of data: Every day, we were receiving *70 thousand data points*. Why weren't we getting 270k? Because our focus was on retail store employees—not warehouse, corporate, or Kmart folks at this stage. For the people we surveyed daily, we had a participation rate of around 75 percent.

Once we started getting that flood of data, we're like: "Holy smokes! What do we do with all of this?" First, we let the data run a while so we could establish baselines or what we called "set points" for different stores. We soon discovered that energy levels in California were simply higher than those in Minnesota in the winter. Duh. So, we tuned the system to show us variations against the local set point.

We had a really small budget, so what we focused on were the locations where people were largely exhausted and those where they were full of energy. We didn't focus on the middle.

Our hypothesis was that if people are exhausted, there will be a poor customer experience at that store, sales will go down, and turnover will increase. The opposite would be true for stores where people were energized.

Pretty soon, we saw anomalies pop up: *We've had a steady number in Baltimore then Whoa! What's going on there!* We had someone go to that store and found out that they had a manager change and the new manager was toxic. We did an intervention. In another city, the daily data would go crazy, and we'd discover details as granular as the local bus routes had changed. Several employees now could not get to work in a reasonable time, so they were being written up and were stressed.

We suddenly had an unbelievable, real-time window into unusual activities happening in any location across the vast system. What's important to notice is we were not being given answers—we were getting questions: "What's going on in St. Louis this last week?" The system highlighted the questions, and we followed up to find the answers.

> *The system highlighted the questions, and we followed up to find the answers.*

Our work in this area ended up being written about in a publication by the Massachusetts Institute of Technology. My colleagues later became head of all global digital for Disney, and head of analytics for Google.

If all that is not impressive enough for you, get this: As I said, we had five possible choices or emojis for energy levels. Actually, there was a hidden sixth option we unexpectedly discovered in the data: "I'm not going to tell you anymore."

To explain, let's say someone fluctuated between higher and lower energy levels over time. That's normal. But if that person—who had been regularly answering the energy question—suddenly stopped answering it, our data showed that they would leave the company within five weeks. It was a near certainty. That was the sixth hidden option that basically said: "I'm done with you people." That was the power of thinking outside the box, collecting a ton of data, and diving into what it all meant. It gave us a finger on the pulse like nothing else, and it couldn't be any fresher, because it was today's data.

Another thing we found was that working hard was not correlated with exhaustion. Some people would be slammed but had high energy. We'd hear things like: "So many customers coming in today. It was so much fun! We helped a lot of people." We'd also hear the opposite, where they were having a hard time with their manager and it was reflected in a day that dragged on forever.

It didn't just work at Sears

When I went to Guild, I introduced both concepts to the other leadership. We had 750 employees and were a fast-moving startup—the opposite of Sears. This time, I told them I wanted to do a weekly survey of energy levels, plus three other questions:

1. A question on something that matters, based on what's going on right now in the company.
2. A question from the survey where people had indicated we needed to change something. For example, we knew we wanted to improve around: "I feel safe to take risks at work," because it was a low score that statistically pulled all engagement down. So, we asked such questions periodically to check on improvement, and to target specific interventions.
3. A fun question, like: "What's your favorite ice cream flavor?"

You should have seen the looks I got. Like, *Why did we hire this guy?* They HATED the idea, but I knew I had the data and experience about how this stuff worked. I said: "Trust me. Just trust me."

At first, I was only focused on tracking participation, because in a smaller company, we needed to work harder to get statistically valid numbers. That meant we needed to give people time to see that the survey wasn't going away, and that we were asking good questions.

A few leaders asked me: "Why aren't my people participating?" I said: "I don't know. You tell me."

After a while, I gave the leaders a list of all leaders ranked by participation rate. Most of the numbers were good, but a few leaders asked me: "Why aren't my people participating?" I said: "I don't know. You tell me." Two weeks later, participation rates went way up. Then the leaders wanted details on the question scores. I told them the scores didn't yet matter because we needed to get to statistical significance.

Once I had valid energy numbers, I sent that list to leaders. Once again, some leaders asked me: "Why are my energy numbers so low?" and I'd say: "You tell me." I also offered to do focus groups for the really low-scoring areas.

We did this process for a year. Energy levels went way up. We measured engagement through a survey, and our scores were up for the first time in three years. In fact, they were up seven points in the period when tech companies were down by an average of ten points.

I've seen this system work in multiple industries and sectors. I've been asked what I would do if I were dropped into an organization and had to take a first step toward figuring out where they were on the employee experience spectrum. I'd first implement this energy pulse survey.

So many possible metrics!

We've mainly been discussing the sort of metrics where you ask someone to respond. It takes careful planning to design those questions in such a way that you avoid the most common problems we listed above. The effort is worth it, and also necessary if you're going to evaluate whether your EX efforts are paying off.

There's a whole different class of metrics that also can help with your evaluations—direct measurements. You don't need to encourage people to participate in a survey but can determine these metrics using other means.

Here are a few examples:

If we improved the job interview experience, we can measure the job offer acceptance rate directly.

Participation rates are an excellent indicator, positively or negatively, especially when you earlier established a baseline. It could be participation in referring others to apply for a job; or involvement in weekly events; and so on.

For emails, open rates and click-through rates can be useful indicators of a change in engagement. When the medium is video, it's easy to measure how long individuals spend watching the video, where they bail out, and even if they "scrub" back to re-watch something.

Turnover is an interesting measurement, because there are two kinds: regrettable and non-regrettable. If you lose someone who has been underperforming for a while, that's a non-regrettable example. On the other hand, if you're trying to retain different cohorts like early employees, under-represented employees (by gender, age, ethnicity, and so on), you might track all these regrettable turnover numbers separately.

Speaking of metrics, the next chapter has many examples of how powerful metrics can be in an organization.

Chapter Summary

We highlighted the ineffectiveness of typical annual engagement surveys as a "snapshot in time."

A "metric" is the dimension and a "measurement" is the data point.

We listed nine considerations for getting useful information, and how it's important to avoid relying *only* on surveys. You also must establish baselines, ensure safety for honest feedback, review for bias, ask frequently but not excessively, get granular, wait for statistical significance, and promptly act on what you learn.

We listed our seven favorite questions of all time:

1. Why did you join?
2. Why do you stay?
3. What do you love?
4. Why would you leave?
5. What's getting in your way?
6. Would you agree or disagree with the following statement: "For what I put into my work, I believe the organization gives back equal or greater value to my life." (More on this in Chapter 15.)
7. "How are you feeling right now?"

The story about Sears was powerful, where an "energy pulse" system (employees selecting emojis on time clocks) provided real-time leading indicators of store issues and even predicted employee attrition. This energy pulse concept was successfully adapted at Guild, showing how it works across different industries and company sizes.

Direct measurements are important (for example, job offer acceptance rates, participation rates, turnover). They are another class of metrics that don't rely on surveys but provide valuable evaluation data.

13

A Conversation with Greg Pryor

Turning Experience into Intelligence and Then into Impact

Background

If there's one person who helped elevate employee experience from a feel-good HR initiative to a CEO-level business imperative, it's Greg Pryor. We have long admired Greg's work, especially during his time at Workday, where he wasn't just ahead of the curve—he was helping redraw it.

Greg has been a pioneer in shaping how we define and measure the employee experience—making it tangible, trackable, and tied to performance and engagement in ways even the most numbers-driven executives can rally behind. He pushed the conversation beyond perks and sentiment into strategy and systems, helping organizations see experience as a lever for business value.

We've had the privilege of learning with and from Greg over the years, and his influence is everywhere—from how we think about culture design to how we elevate employee voice at the highest levels. In this interview, you'll get a glimpse of the clarity, passion, and practicality that have made Greg a true legend in this space. He's not just a legend, he's a great friend.

Could you please tell us a little about your background and how you landed where you are?

I'm actually a second-generation talent and leadership development person. My dad did this work back in the day. So I feel like I definitely have had the incredible privilege of knowing people in this space literally since I was a teenager, attending events. I majored in business and organizational communications in school.

I grew up in the New York area, so I've got a little bit of what you might call New York elbows. But I've spent a long time in California, and the vision and peacefulness of the Bay Area has rubbed off on me. I try to bring both energies to what I do.

Anyway, I spent 10 years at Accenture in consulting. I then moved to Merrill Lynch, in the very classic New York human capital space, which was interesting. I was at Merrill Lynch in 2008. As you may recall, 2008 was not a great time to be in New York City financial services, right in the middle of the financial meltdown.

I had the incredible privilege to meet Steven Rice, who was CHRO at Juniper Networks, and also Scott Kriens, who was the CEO. Juniper is one of the biggest names in computer networking solutions and cloud infrastructure.

"I have a vision for Juniper to be a multigenerational community and company where people can make the impossible possible."

When I interviewed with Scott, I asked him what he wants his legacy at Juniper to be. I'll never forget his answer: "I have a vision for Juniper to be a multigenerational community and company where people can make the impossible possible." Nothing about networks, internet protocols, security solutions, and all the stuff Juniper is world famous for, even though Scott was a brilliant technologist by training. It was about the employee experience and how it tied to company goals—making the impossible possible.

I was telling my wife, Tammy, about my meetings at Juniper and I said I was blown away by Scott Kriens. She said: "You're not blown away by anyone." I explained how he had this incredible vision and was so thoughtfully grounded in the importance of culture and values and creating a space where people could unlock. At the end of our catch-up call, Tammy said: "It sounds like we're moving to California."

When you moved to Juniper, what was your role there?

I reported to Steven, the CHRO. My role was to create the conditions where a multigenerational community could make the impossible possible. To be more specific, our company was involved in not just incremental improvements; we were looking for fundamentally new technology that represented breakthroughs. We needed to create specific conditions by which you could unleash that level of capability, where people could unlock their best work.

Scott and Steven set the direction. It was my responsibility to build the programs, practices, and principles that would realize that vision.

How did you go about creating those conditions for success?

We took a step back, and we asked ourselves: "What would it look like to enable people to be high performers?" We came up with five fundamental conditions or factors that—if we were to create these conditions for people—we could unlock that high performance.

> First, people need to **understand what their contribution is**, and the organization needs to be clear minded: "This is what success looks like in your job."
>
> The second is this idea of your **personal capabilities**: your skills, experience, energy, and the resilience you bring to work.
>
> The third is your **career interests**: How does the contribution you're making and the capabilities you're using align with your career interests and aspirations?
>
> The fourth is **connections**: What are the relationships that enable you to be successful, and how do you think about those?
>
> The fifth one is **compensation**: Do you feel fairly recognized and rewarded for your contribution?

We got to work and focused on building a set of aligned and integrated practices that sent a message to employees that we actually cared about those five conditions being true.

Our goal was to build all of our talent practices around those five conditions. But when we compared them to our performance management practice, they were completely out of alignment. We got to work and focused on building a set of aligned and integrated practices that sent a message to employees that we actually cared about those five conditions being true.

In a sense, these conditions seem really obvious. But traditionally, HR organizations have way over-complicated things, and they also very rarely have put employees at the center and said: "The outcome we're trying to create here is extraordinary performance of individuals." You need to start with that.

The great thing at Juniper was we were big enough to matter yet still small enough to experiment.

When did you join Workday?

After spending about five years at Juniper, I met some amazing people at Workday including my very good friends, Leighanne Levensaler and Ashley Goldsmith. The company was about 2,000 people and was on a really fast growth curve. There were nearly 20,000 employees when I left.

What was your role at Workday?

It was to help scale the company without sacrificing their culture. It was a challenge because 50 percent of our leaders were either new to leading or new to the company.

We saw some early warning signs that we needed to work harder on our culture. One of those signs came in the form of a couple of Glassdoor comments that were the first time we had ever seen negative comments from employees. Then we had a moment during the company picnic, when a young engineer tweeted out: "Epic fail. Ran out of hamburgers at the company picnic. Have to wait."

We had somehow gotten to a place where we're at a picnic, which should have been about support for one another and gratitude. Instead, the fact that you weren't getting your hamburgers on time was something worthy of tweeting out.

We had an executive meeting about that moment, and ironically it turned out to be a blessing for us. Workday revisits that moment every year at its annual People Leadership Summit, and posts the tweet as a cautionary tale and call to action, as in: "This will not happen again," not in a punishment sense but about how we need to be ever mindful of the culture we're creating.

One of the things we did was create Feedback Fridays. Every Friday, we asked our entire employee base two questions, drawn from 34 questions. They were all related to the five factors I mentioned earlier. We wanted a series of questions that would measure employees' experience, and we would hold our leaders accountable for the experience they were creating. Asking two at a time meant it was easy to answer, and we'd cover them all in every quarter, so we could see trends.

Didn't Workday partner with the Great Place to Work Institute?

Yes we did. Michael Bush was CEO there, and we really liked some of their research. One concept we adopted was their Five Levels of Leadership, which was based on research of massive numbers of surveys across organizations. I can recommend Michael's book, *A Great Place to Work For All*.[1]

Level 1 is the Unintentional Leader who's thrown into the deep end of managing with no effective training. This person is toxic, and the common reaction by employees to this style of leadership is: "I don't get paid enough to put up with this."

Level 2 is the Hit or Miss Leader. It's a little better but depending on the day and the topic, employees can feel OK or feel terrible while dealing with this person. It's like coming to work each day and playing Russian Roulette.

Level 3 is the Transactional Leader. This is someone who's making an effort, but it's more toward checking things off a list and not about building relationships.

The Level 4 person is a Good Leader. Most people are lucky to ever have such a leader because they inspire you to go the extra mile for them.

Level 5 is what Michael calls the "For All Leader." They're not perfect, but they are humble, inspirational, and incredibly effective.

---

[1] Bush, Michael C., and Great Place to Work. *A Great Place to Work for All: Better for Business, Better for People, Better for the World*. Oakland: Berrett-Koehler Publishers, Incorporated, 2018.

When we first applied the idea of using levels of leadership to our leaders, it was not an easy pill to swallow. We quickly pivoted to measuring the team's employee experience, which had a level of both abstraction and accountability that was received much better.

Though manager experience mattered most, we created accountability at varying levels of organization leadership, including individual offices, all the way to the company level. We had a company OKR based on the percentage of employees having a level 4 or 5 experience that would place us among the top companies in the world.

Every quarter we provided a scoreboard to leaders. It said things like: "Greg, your team is having a level 4 experience. This is what that means, and here is one thing you can do to improve…."

We tied the five factors of our talent management strategy to the feedback our employees were giving. We also analyzed each office and each function, so we could look at it multidimensionally. If any leader was below what we would call a level 3 or transactional experience, they would get personalized coaching. Aneel Bhusri, CEO, was very open to this. He said that if you went more than two quarters without creating this level of experience, you probably were not going to be a leader at Workday for long.

The minimum expectation was to have created at least that transactional experience. If people were good but maybe not just great at people leadership, we'd find a role where they could be successful. Aneel joked that if they were not a good leader, we'd get them a job at Oracle. (Just a little competitive ribbing in jest.)

All of our leadership development programs were focused on that system, and we had accountability measurements every Friday.

Every year we celebrated those leaders who had the highest levels of performance. It was the biggest celebration that Workday did, outside of celebrating its customers.

How did your system work out?

I love our friends at Covey.[2] They talk about the idea of how a sports coach will have

> *Every year we celebrated those leaders who had the highest levels of performance. It was the biggest celebration that Workday did, outside of celebrating its customers.*

---

[2] https://www.franklincovey.com/

a million stats on everything, but there also is the big scoreboard that answers the question: "Are we winning or losing?"

We definitely wanted both. We wanted to let every leader know how they were doing overall and in detail, and we also wanted the big outcome measurements.

We monitored these metrics like crazy. For example, we would immediately know if there was a hotspot, and could see hotspots by team. We didn't look by employee, but we did look by function and by career level.

We tailored our involvement to the situations we encountered. Sometimes it was as simple as reaching out to a particular functional leader and asking what's going on. Other times I'd get on a plane to an office in Europe, for example, because we saw a precipitous drop in some metrics.

What was the issue with that European office and what did you do?

We wanted to create a great place to work for all, regardless of whether you were in the Paris or Toronto office; regardless of your gender; if you were new or a long-time Workday employee; and so on. I thought about this index as being similar to a smoke detector: Once it was tripped, we could send a person to investigate and get more context.

We didn't just measure people's views in the office against that office's baseline, but we also wanted to measure everything against the high water mark—which might be the Minneapolis office, for example.

I did fly to that European office, because that office was having a materially lower experience according to the measures. We checked with the Great Place to Work Institute, which has enormous data sets by country and other factors. It was not just a local culture thing, but something else was going on.

That meeting actually led us to establish a practice that still exists today: There is an executive accountable for every major office in the world. Of course, we already had people in each office who were responsible, but we also had this executive who was saying, "I'm going to be your office sponsor and am taking responsibility to be your ally. I'm independently responsible for looking each quarter at the results at your office."

"I'm going to be your office sponsor and am taking responsibility to be your ally. I'm independently responsible for looking each quarter at the results at your office."

We gave each senior leader in the company responsibility for three offices. I had Toronto, Minneapolis, and Victoria Island in Canada. We would visit those offices and would be incredibly transparent about sharing the results of the office compared to the company—this is where we're doing well; this is where we're not. It was my responsibility to work with the more senior leaders at the office. It was really powerful.

Didn't you guys do some groundbreaking work in going from annual engagement surveys to the concept of doing a pulse?

Yes. As far as I know, we were the first to go from the common annual survey to creating Feedback Friday in 2017, where we asked questions every week. As I said earlier, we rotated the questions, so it was easy to fill out. Over time, it covered a lot of issues, and we got data ranging from weekly to quarterly in frequency.

And let me tell you, it was not a walk in the park to get the executive team to go along with this idea. I remember the meeting so clearly. There were 30 people at the meeting where I proposed this "pulse" approach. In between some pretty salty language, a few people made it clear that I was nuts. "You're *not* going to do that!" was one of the comments.

My natural instinct was to push back and stand my ground, but luckily for me, I paused before doing that. Then our head of user experience said: "People do this on Yelp every day. This is the way work happens now. We need to lean into this." I was grateful to this person for having the courage to support this heretical idea. I said, "Look, if we suffer survey fatigue from this, we'll change it." So we went ahead.

Fast forward two years, and once a week was not enough. When the pandemic hit, people's experiences were changing daily, if not faster. Phil Wilburn, who still looks after people analytics for Workday, said: "Thank goodness we put this in place when we did. We were prepared to measure what was happening to our employees nearly in real time in the midst of COVID and could respond just as quickly."

It's the power of having continuous data versus just asking questions every once in a while. First, it gives you a really solid baseline, and then it allows you to see variations and ask questions about what's going on. After all, we had a customer experience team that continuously listened to our customers; why wouldn't we have an employee experience team that continuously listened to our employees? It was that simple.

Who are others that have influenced you?

Ann Rhoades was one of my amazing mentors at Juniper and became head of people at Southwest and then JetBlue. She introduced me to the idea of a brand system: Who we are on the inside is who we are on the outside. It's either a virtuous cycle or a vicious cycle.

We had a customer experience team that continuously listened to our customers; why wouldn't we have an employee experience team that continuously listened to our employees?

The senior leadership team at Workday absolutely got that. It was Workday founders Dave Duffield and Aneel's first principle that happy employees lead to happy customers. We can't directly control our impact on thousands and thousands of customers, but we can support a relatively small group of leaders who can in turn enable our 10,000 employees. You see Ann's work in how Southwest and JetBlue were, back in the day: You can look at the quality of your flight experience and can look at the engagement of the flight attendants and the desk staff, and you can trace those experiences together.

You described how you took a leap to gather so much more data than was traditionally available through annual surveys, and how valuable that was. Despite the value of that, did you have detractors?

Not really, once we got going. In fact, we ended up purchasing a company that now does Feedback Friday for Workday. We also had gotten accustomed to having the near-real-time data. Once you have it, you can't imagine going backward and saying, *The company and world are continuously changing, but I'm OK with not having a current view.* We had tied the people analytics data to performance, retention, and promotion goals. It became part of the fundamental operation of the company.

We learned a lot about the conditions for high performance. For example, Workday had a very robust way for employees to give each other feedback. We could see very clearly who was giving feedback to whom, and how they were supporting one another. We saw very high correlations between the frequency of giving employees feedback, and their performance and retention.

We also could see how central someone was in the network and used that information to choose who went to leadership development programs, because we could see the centrality of their influence on ideas within the company. We developed influence analytics within the company to say these people had a higher likelihood of effecting the type of change we wanted to see in the organization, based on their connections within the company. It was very sophisticated stuff that drove material business results.

We did a quarterly infographic to the whole company: "Here's what we learned about these questions we asked, and here are the trends we're seeing." We tried to make it interesting and engaging.

Once you establish the habit, it's a habit. But it can be a lot of work to get it to become one. The company has had a pretty steady weekly response rate of 75 to 78 percent. That happens when people see it's immediately converted into action and accountability. If you don't have that accountability, the response rate drops. They think, *Why am I doing this?*

How much data did you need before it became significant?

> *Once you get that first solid report back, people pay attention—especially the people whose units rank at the bottom. No one likes to be at the bottom.*

We needed about four months of data before we had enough statistically solid data that we could generate insights. Before then, it was more of a "trust me" matter, where you use relationship capital to get that data. But once you get that first solid report back, people pay attention—especially the people whose units rank at the bottom. No one likes to be at the bottom.

The other thing we did that worked out well was we rolled out the pulse effort first to the teams of the top 450 leaders, then to all employees covered by our remaining 2,000 people leaders. We didn't want to make employees the guinea pigs.

Also, Aneel was very honest and transparent about the results relating to his direct reports. He told everyone: "Here's what the most senior people in the company are telling me I could be better at." Robynne, our CFO, did the same thing. She shared her results with the entire leadership community and said what she was working on to improve.

For example, people in the finance organization indicated there wasn't much in the way of fun in their jobs. She said, "We're going to try Funance Fridays because I know our work is hard, and I've heard you. The engineering teams have their 'May the Fourth Be With You' Day, so I'm asking you to close the books on Funance Fridays." The tone starts at the top.

Let's say an organization has someone at the top whose tone is not conducive to great employee experiences. Can some of these principles get embedded in an organization anyway?

I think so. Maybe there's a leader somewhere else in the organization who's a level 4 or level 5 individual. They can do this kind of communication in some fashion. They can ask for that feedback, because they won't otherwise know how to get better.

I was doing a simple form of Feedback Fridays 10 years before I came to Workday. It was around a coffee at the end of the week, before we went home. I'd ask the team: "How was our week? What can I do better? Where were we good and where are we bad?" You simply have to do it, if you're going to be a good leader and engage your team. It's very doable. It's a lot easier if it's a company-wide initiative, of course. But at the end of the day, what matters is that you get feedback about what you can do differently.

At the end of the day, what matters is that you get feedback about what you can do differently.

I think a form of this is going to happen with AI. Before AI, we had already picked up the pace at which we listened to what employees were saying—by asking them weekly and in some cases, daily. Now AI will pick up the pace at which we can do something about it. Instead of having to manually crunch lots of data, soon there will be an AI agent that instantly creates a report indicating what's happening in the Toledo office, and it will suggest an action plan. It will alert the right people, enable someone to enroll in a program, curate content for the program, and more.

It's going to be such a game changer for organizations that recognize the potential and do something about it. The companies that don't understand this will be left behind. And it's almost here.

Thanks, Greg, for your time and the many insights you shared!
You're very welcome.

Chapter Summary

Greg was influenced by Juniper's CEO, who focused on creating conditions for a multigenerational community where employees could "make the impossible possible."

Greg identified five fundamental conditions or what he refers to as the Five Factors for High Performance: Contribution, Capabilities, Career Interests, Connections, and Compensation and Recognition, which are aligned and enabled through the talent practices around them.

Workday pioneered "Feedback Fridays," a weekly pulse survey asking two rotating questions from a bank of 34, to continuously measure employee experience and hold leaders accountable.

Workday partnered with the Great Place to Work Institute, adopting their "Five Levels of Leadership" to evaluate manager effectiveness, making it personal and consumable and tying it to EX outcomes.

They used people analytics to identify "hotspots" of experience by function, career level, and demographics, enabling targeted interventions like flying to Europe to address specific issues.

The shift from annual surveys to weekly pulses was a major move that provided real-time data, proving invaluable during the pandemic for quick responses to changing employee experiences.

Greg connects EX to the business outcomes through the simple yet powerful idea that happy employees lead to happy customers, a first principle at Workday, and he mentioned how AI will further accelerate the ability to identify and act on employee feedback in smarter and more specific ways.

PART VI
Celebrate/Extend

14

A Conversation with Michelle Bonfilio

The Emotional Core of Employee Experience Design

Background

Michelle and I (Mark) worked together at three different companies. I have seen Michelle's career and her strategic approach to HR/EX blossom over the years. I've been so impressed with how she has shaped the people and culture of the companies she worked with and the employees she co-created with.

Michelle joined Dean, Samantha, and me on an incredible quest to Bhutan in 2024 where we learned from the Bhutanese about compassion and purpose, and how to bring these ideas into the workplace through Employee Experience. We were moved by Michelle's stories in her current role, and knew she would add much to this book. You will learn a lot from her conversation.

To start, what's your current company?

I am the Chief People Officer for Help at Home, LLC. We're the largest national provider of home care services to the elderly population, with more than 60,000 employees. We call our employees "caregivers." We currently operate in 11 states. We're rapidly expanding, following the growth of the aging demographic across the US. Help at Home's mission is to enable individuals to have Great Days with independence and dignity at home. Through our services and programs, our clients enjoy Great Days and Meaningful Moments through dedicated, relationship-based, in-home personal care.

What did you originally want to do?

That was the big question I had for myself when I graduated from college. I honestly didn't know what I wanted to do from a career perspective. When I started college, I had every intention of going into medicine and majored in biological sciences. About halfway through, I switched to psychology; I was fascinated more by the study of the brain versus the study of the body.

For my entire collegiate career at UC Davis, I worked at an on-campus eatery called "The Coffee House." It wasn't some little operation—we had hundreds of employees. By my senior year, I was a manager. My job included hiring, onboarding, and training.

I graduated during a recession. One of my aunts was in human resources at the time. She introduced me to the leader of talent acquisition at The Good Guys, a California-based consumer-electronics retail chain. My first job was recruiting assistant. And that role unexpectedly launched me into the human capital space, largely in the retail and consumer packaged goods (CPG) sectors.

Prior to Help at Home, I served as CHRO for Petco, Health & Wellness Company, Inc. Focusing on the "whole health" of pets was central to Petco's mission. One of our growth strategies in support of that mission was providing veterinary services to pet parents, through both in-store veterinary hospitals and mobile vet clinics. A significant part of our workforce were veterinarians and animal para-health professionals.

Learning about what mattered most to individuals entering veterinary medicine was central to supporting our growth. I really got to understand the values and needs of DVMs, veterinary technicians, and coordinators—why they chose to enter the profession, what they wanted in their career experience, and what were the most difficult and rewarding parts of their work.

Understanding all of this was instrumental in shaping how we crafted our recruitment and retention plans; after all, we had to sell this workforce on why they should join a retailer as opposed to an independent veterinary practice.

What made you join Petco?

I got a call in 2018 about the Petco opportunity from someone in my network. She was a former CHRO herself, and she knew the CEO was rebuilding his executive team. Petco was struggling at the time; it didn't have a lot of differentiation in the market versus PetSmart and others. Petco had approximately 29,000 employees in 1,500 stores across all 50 states.

As I got to know the CEO, we spent a lot of time talking about the importance of differentiating the experience of partners, which is what we called our employees. We wanted to focus on the "whole health" of the Petco workforce, making intentional investments in how employees lived their lives, as well as creating the right working environment within our stores, distribution centers, and home offices.

When I started, employee engagement scores were very low and attrition was very high, even by retail norms. Our workforce was demoralized. I was one of several new executives that started within a relatively short period. Within a year, we collectively worked to get the business back on track and set up for very strong financial performance and expansion in the subsequent years.

When I reflect on that experience, the thing I am most proud of—and actually humbled by—is how we re-engineered the entire partner experience. Just as company performance stabilized, the pandemic hit. We knew we had to double-down on our employee experience commitments. As a senior team, we believed deeply in servant leadership; our collective responsibility was to serve our workforce. We knew that our ability to successfully connect with pet parents was through our employee base. We created a really cool set of strategies designed to demonstrate to our partners that they weren't just working for us—at the end of the day, we were there to make their roles as simple, easy, and elegant as possible.

> *We created a really cool set of strategies designed to demonstrate to our partners that they weren't just working for us—at the end of the day, we were there to make their roles as simple, easy, and elegant as possible.*

We came out the other side of the pandemic, turning the business around with a workforce that—by the time I left four years later—had engagement scores in the 80th percentile. Our retention numbers improved exponentially, particularly on the retail front.

One thing we did to make that happen was to focus on the demographics of our workforce. Demographically, our workforce was largely female and predominantly Millennial and Gen Z. We were very intentional about looking at life stages and what was important to those cohorts around everything from benefits, to how they wanted to learn on the job, and what was important to them from a career development perspective. We tested, learned, and tested some more. It was a fun ride.

When was the first time that you were exposed to the concept of employee experience?

I worked for Gap, Inc for almost 10 years. I joined them in 2005 and in 2008 transitioned to a division at the time called Gap Inc Direct (GID), the company's emergent global ecommerce business unit.

Within GID, I worked closely with our product management, customer experience, and customer relationship management functions. The teams were looking at ways to make the shopping experience as easy as possible for the customer—how to "surprise and delight" them. We wanted to understand the moments when a customer would decide to jettison the store or the ecommerce site without making a purchase. Experiences like not being able to find a particular size or color of a garment, or standing in too long of a line for a cashier, and many others. We created customer journey maps of all these, so that we could identify ways to make shopping easier and more delightful.

At one point, a light bulb went off for me where I was like, *we can actually be looking at the employee experience the same way*. We should be understanding what gets in the way of an employee being able to smoothly go from the recruitment process, to onboarding effectively, to contributing to their fullest potential, and so on.

> *A light bulb went off for me where I was like, we can actually be looking at the employee experience the same way. We should be understanding what gets in the way of an employee being able to smoothly go from the recruitment process, to onboarding effectively, to contributing to their fullest potential, and so on.*

I sat down with the heads of product management and CRM and their leadership teams. We talked about how we did all this analysis from a customer perspective, and how we might do some beta testing of the same concept with our workforce. We were just a small division within a large company—about 1,500 employees and nearly $2B in revenue, whereas Gap Inc overall had approximately 135,000 employees and more than $15B in revenues. It was relatively safe to test within our division.

We started to do some testing. One challenge we faced was our ability to directly compete for top-tier technology talent. GID was located in San Francisco. At that time, both established and start-up technology companies were beginning to migrate their office footprints from Silicon Valley up into San Francisco and across into the East Bay. Though we liked to believe we were a technology company that happened to sell clothes, versus operating as a tech division within a retailer, we knew we were hard pressed to vie for the same tech talent pools gravitating to the lure of Silicon Valley. We couldn't be competitive on a pure cash basis, and certainly not from an equity perspective, versus the giant public companies or sexy start-ups with their outsized stock offerings.

We asked ourselves: "What should we think about software engineers and data architects who might work in one of those environments where staff is expected to work crazy hours, because that was just the culture? How many of these people might be looking for better balance, either because they want to spend time with their families, or they have outside interests they want to pursue, but their existing environment doesn't allow them to do so?" What if we built a recruitment campaign around well-being and intentionally went after folks in these companies that we knew were burning out their talent? We could provide more flexibility around scheduling, while also guaranteeing innovative product and engineering work.

We were already rolling out what we called a "results only workplace" concept—we eliminated this notion of having to be in the office Monday through Friday, nine to five. It was about giving autonomy to employees to determine when, where, and how to work, creating schedules within the construct of their broader life commitments. As long as work got done, with the same expectations around quality, deadlines, etc., it didn't really matter when and where employees were. We're going to measure staff on their results and not when they were in the office. It feels so funny to talk about it now, but back in 2010, that was not how people were working. Everyone was in the office because you simply had to be there. It was all about butts in seats.

How did you get the word out about your new approach?

A lot of it was how we branded ourselves from a talent acquisition perspective. After we had some experience, we put together some specific branding campaigns where we produced videos with snippets of our employees talking about how this affected them positively.

We interviewed leaders who talked about how it increased the talent pipeline and engagement. We didn't see any noticeable drop in our ability to meet our KPIs or deliver on our financial targets, despite having this flexible approach.

What sort of metrics did you focus on?

We looked at things like timeliness of response. We didn't have the same technology and sophistication that we have today for tracking such things. If we didn't have people working on the same floor during the same hours, did it slow down decision-making or deliverable dates?

We looked at the burnout factor, because one thing we were concerned about was by moving to this environment, were we unintentionally encouraging people to work more hours?

We analyzed our overall retention. Some of the early learning was that there was some breakage around ensuring real clarity about goals. We got early feedback that we needed to make sure we created more consistency for people to understand what was expected of them.

We spent time on how leaders monitored and measured performance; whether employees were getting feedback in a timely manner; and if they were not on track, how employees could get help.

One challenge was to create more of a continuous feedback loop, not just within teams, but between leaders and their employees. It was a lot of testing and learning. We felt like we were constantly beta testing. Every couple of weeks, we made something that we thought was a little more efficient, and then we'd study the data we got back and make the next adjustment.

> *Every couple of weeks, we made something that we thought was a little more efficient, and then we'd study the data we got back and make the next adjustment.*

Did your efforts cause some envy in other business units?

I don't know about envy, but we did see an increase in internal applicants pretty significantly.

When was the first time you felt that you could put in place the people and culture strategy that you wanted to implement?

It wasn't when I first became a CHRO. I had that title at a company where they didn't have that role before. It was an interesting learning experience for me, because I underestimated how difficult it would be to institute a people and culture strategy in a company that previously hadn't had one.

It was a heavily unionized workforce, and the notion of focusing on people from a strategic perspective was not how they looked at the business. It was more about having a job for the long term in exchange for loyalty. There wasn't a discussion around our business strategies, what was getting in the way of our ability to execute against those strategies, and what were the people-related elements of the strategies that we could fix. I didn't thread the needle very well or align on the right KPIs with my executive peers.

What was the pushback you were getting?

It was more like: "That's not HR's role. Your role is to administer the policies." That was not who I was, so I told them I would find someone who could do that all day long for them.

It was when I went to Petco that I really felt like I had ownership, authority, and also buy-in from my peers and the board. We were able to develop a really comprehensive approach to people and culture. It wasn't always smooth sailing, but nothing ever is.

> We were able to develop a really comprehensive approach to people and culture. It wasn't always smooth sailing, but nothing ever is.

Knowing what you know now about organizations, what advice would you give to somebody who's thinking of joining a certain organization, and they're interviewing—how do they determine if the organization has the employee experience mindset, instead of finding out the hard way that they don't have one?

So much of that is about asking the right questions about their business strategy. I always start there. Where is the organization today? Where do they see themselves three years from now? Five years from now? Help me understand the segment you're in and the competitors. What are the headwinds and tailwinds? What plans do you have in place to grow revenues from where you are to your targets over a three-year period?

Through that set of questions, I'm listening for what they say are the inputs to achieving those growth goals.

I'm not impressed if they say they need to double their workforce over three years to get from revenue X to revenue Y. What I'm listening for are deeper attributes about people, like the type of demographic they've traditionally hired may be such that they need to hire or train for certain other capabilities; they need to think about where to pull talent from; what their organizing principles need to be; and so on.

> *I never lead with: "Tell me about your people strategy." I want to come in and talk about where they're headed purely from an economic and market perspective.*

I poke under the covers quite a bit, but here's the thing, and it's really important—I never lead with: "Tell me about your people strategy." I want to come in and talk about where they're headed purely from an economic and market perspective. What do you view as the detractors and accelerants to get you there? I mean, it always ends up coming back to people, capabilities, and culture, so we eventually have that conversation. But if I can create alignment around what our shared business objectives are, then it's easier for me to say: "OK, now let me start talking to you as a practitioner of people and as a coach on culture. Let's talk about the different attributes in those categories that might be accelerants or detractors so we can achieve those business goals."

Didn't you have an uphill challenge when you joined Petco?

We did. When I started, our engagement scores were really low, and there was a high degree of mistrust of senior management. The workforce didn't feel that they were being heard.

It just so happened that the new Chief Stores Officer and I started within the same month. We intentionally spent our first six months traveling to different locations. Every time we were in a new location, we held a series of partner roundtables. They were always scheduled early in the morning, prior to store operating hours, so we brought coffee and donuts.

We asked them three specific questions. One was an icebreaker, like what's your favorite holiday movie or something like that. Then we asked: "What do you love about Petco?" and "What's getting in the way of serving the customer?"

Through just those questions, we gathered so much information! Some of it was about the employee experience, and some was about the customer experience and things like our product assortment. We got some feedback that wasn't relevant, but we also got a lot of actionable feedback. We took that back and began to take action on it right away.

From there, we started to create a little momentum, particularly with our field employees. They began to say things that indicated: *OK, they're listening to us. We'll provide more feedback.* We then stood up a series of employee advisory groups that served as extensions to my team. Any time we were thinking about a new challenge, we were in lockstep with this advisory group to say: "OK, here's what we've heard as the problem statement. Let's discuss ways to solve it. Let's pressure test the top two or three solutions. How can we actually take it from inception to practical application across 1,500 stores...."

These advisory folks felt really invested in the solutions. We made it clear that we were asking for their feedback and wanted them involved in the solutions. We'd test the ideas, and if they worked, we'd not be the ones up on stage. Instead, we'd give credit where credit was due, which was to whatever group of employees raised the issue or were part of the solution. It just became how we did things—not only around employee experience, but also how we looked at our merchandising strategies, marketing strategies, the efficiencies of the store footprint . . . you name it. It was so powerful.

How difficult was it to set up the advisory groups?

At first, employees were like, "Why are you asking?" There was some initial skepticism, as in: "Are we going to get in trouble if we say something is broken?" We had to be really diligent to say "No, we're asking because you're closest to the customer, and we need your opinions." It took some months before people realized we meant what we said.

How did you choose the advisory group members? And what would be an example of a suggestion that came up that worked and that you wouldn't have otherwise known about?

Our Next Gen Advisory Group was made up of mid-level leaders that had been identified as being on the succession path to eventually becoming general managers of stores. They were supervisors, assistant managers, and associate managers. We asked people for a twelve-month commitment, because we were pulling them into pretty frequent meetings to go through all this discovery and testing work.

We also had PRGs, or Partner Resource Groups. They represented a broad sample of our population. We wanted the groups to focus less on "fun, food, and famous people." We wanted them to influence our business strategy. These two cohorts ended up becoming really important for us as we developed new solutions.

To answer your question about what's something that we pushed through that we might not have otherwise focused on, I'll answer it slightly differently. One thing we worked on continuously when I was at Petco was our benefits offerings.

When I started, out of a peer group of 24 or 25 companies, we ranked 24th or 25th across all the benchmark categories. We had shitty, shitty benefits. It was awful. It got in our way of being able to attract and retain the people we needed. We finally started to make some significant investments over the following years.

One offering I could never get over the finish line was infertility benefits. Keep in mind that we had a 70 percent female workforce, mainly of child-rearing age. Our executive team just regularly blocked it.

Our women's resource group approached us about helping. They did an incredible job of pulling together a whole set of data. Several of them had their own personal stories that they overlaid into the qualitative and quantitative data around why this would be good for us. This group and my team co-authored a proposal. We took it to the executive team and explained the economics behind this type of benefit and why we needed to do it. That's what got it over the finish line.

We sometimes compare employee experience design as being similar to the person up on stage, spinning plates, where you have to regularly inject energy into the plates to keep them going. Has that been your experience?

At Petco, we were really big on town halls, getting out in front of our workforce in lots of different settings. And we were always branding ourselves. One t-shirt in particular became the mainstay for executives to wear anytime we were standing in front of our population. The shirt logo said, "I'm not confused. I work for you." It was kind of symbolic and as much a way to keep the senior team on the hook as it was a message to employees. We'd put these shirts on, get in front of our workforce, and talk about what was changing and what questions they had.

I share that because when we first started the town halls, things were not so good. In the Q & A, I'd say 95 percent of the questions were around the poor employee experience. I used to joke that I was literally and figuratively in the hot seat because we'd get through these town halls and I'd have to change my shirt, I was so worked up. I was up there, trying to figure out how to address past issues and more importantly, how to get people to believe we were now focused on them. The t-shirt was a small down payment on what we needed to do, which was to prove by our actions that we took our employees' experiences seriously.

After Petco, what attracted you to Health at Home?

I was intrigued by both the business model and especially by the mission of the company. The organization serves the most vulnerable populations who are disadvantaged from a health perspective; predominantly the elderly and disabled communities across the US. We enable these cohorts to live with a degree of independence and vitality in their homes, through having home-health aid. It provides better outcomes for the individual and their families, as well as the broader community, and it lessens the debt incurred by people who don't want institutionalized health care. Statistics show that most people want to age gracefully in their homes for as long as possible.

I was impressed by the CEO and his belief system. He said that the way we care for our caregivers then translates into positive effects on the clients we serve. So much resonated with me.

The way we care for our caregivers then translates into positive effects on the clients we serve.

How different are the challenges at Help at Home, compared with what you experienced at the other places you've worked?

The workforce I now have is quite different from an hourly one that you find at a retailer. For our caregivers, their place of employment is literally someone's home. They don't come to an office or even have a cohort team that works remotely and gets together online.

Their primary connection to the company is through their supervisor. It's a highly independent workforce. We talk about how someone's shift starts as soon as they put their hand on the doorknob and enter someone's home. There's a high degree of shared vulnerability, because you're going into someone's home and you're strangers to each other. There's just this sense of intimacy that's different from any other work environment I've ever been in.

Some of our caregivers work full time, and others work five or seven hours a week. Some of them are licensed, and others are family caregivers—it could be the son, daughter, niece, or nephew caring for the parent, and they're paid to do it. We have so many caregiver situations and motivations, it's a challenge from my perspective to create a single set of offerings that meet the needs of our entire workforce. I work closely with my chief operating officer and our respective teams to more fulsomely understand caregiver experiences that are meaningful and relevant for our demographics, given the diversity of the people who work for us.

One thing he's challenged me on is our overall philosophy about employee experience offerings. I inherited a "one size fits all" model where we didn't look at cohorts or personas. It was one set of benefits, one way to think about career development and skill enhancement, and so on.

Now we're focused on what really matters to the caregiver who works 25, 30, 40 hours a week, but also the ones who work only 5 hours a week. They're going to be different, and we need to ensure that we're addressing both groups, so they want to stay with Help at Home and still give the quality care that we expect them to provide to their clients.

One person on our team has the title of Chief Caregiver Officer. He's been with the company for more than 30 years and has always held caregiver roundtables, kind of like what I did at Petco. He's gathered really awesome feedback, but no one's ever done anything with it! I'm starting to work with him in partnership with our Chief Operating Officer, and we're realizing that we have a *lot* of data. Now we need to package it, determine what the right investments are to make first, and how we tie them back to the quality of care in the community.

We talk about the three C's—Client, Caregiver, Community. It starts with caring for the caregiver, because that ensures they can take care of their clients.

As an example, one thing we've only started to scratch the surface on here is something I also experienced at Petco—compassion fatigue. Pet parents would bring in their pets who had an illness such that there needed to be a discussion around end-of-life decisions.

It's a big part of what a vet has to deal with daily. It took a toll on them and on the veterinary staff, too. We started putting in things around how to get ahead of compassion fatigue, how to recognize when it started to show up, and how to care for that workforce once it did show up.

I see parallels in the home-health industry. A lot of home health agencies focus specifically on what we might call the compliance requirements of providing care: I need to know how to lift someone in and out of a chair; that kind of thing. But no one's training around what to do after a client dies, or needs to move into long-term institutionalized care. What to do when family members might not like having a caregiver around the house. There's a whole realm of emotional management, and it's fundamental to how the caregiver can be effective and also be in this profession long term. Never mind the financials—we're starting to think about what resources we can provide to our caregivers so they can combat compassion fatigue.

How does it show up?

You start to see caregivers call in sick. You see slippage in their care plans. Maybe some complaints come through on the client line.

Is it possible to have an early warning system before you see those signs?

Retailers already do this sort of thing, and we're doing it here now too: It's about teaching supervisors and care managers to have frequent check-ins with their caregivers. We're testing mentorship programs, so caregivers who've been successful with us for a long time can be paired with new caregivers to help them navigate some of these relational elements. We want caregivers to know they're not alone, and don't have to figure things out on their own.

With the challenge you have right now with your 60,000 caregivers, what other listening posts do you have in place for the employee experience?

We are implementing different strategies: We have an internal mobile app for caregivers that we're starting to use as our primary vehicle for communicating with them. We're also building out different pulse surveys to get real-time feedback. Then there is the mentorship I mentioned earlier, and

> *Some people speculate that caregivers won't want to come together for some of these events, but I'm like, "Maybe. Let's try it."*

the roundtables. Some people speculate that caregivers won't want to come together for some of these events, but I'm like, "Maybe. Let's try it."

What's the hardest part of your job?

At the end of the day, we don't see our workforce. They're not in the office, and they're not even on Zoom. For someone in my role, that's really hard.

The second thing is the challenge that most organizations have, and it's what makes employee experience design so rewarding: getting all leaders comfortable with not knowing everything themselves, but being OK with co-designing with employees. It's getting comfortable with regularly saying: "Let's test this. We don't have to commit to anything, but let's test, let's learn." It's not like I'm being met with resistance; it's more like: "We never thought of it this way."

What would you say is the reason employee experience is not a household word and why every company doesn't do it by default?

> *"Let me demonstrate to you that if we improve retention by X percent or if we improve this aspect of the employee experience by Y percent, this is what the business result will look like."*

I think it's up to CHROs to quantify the impact of employee experience. We need to be able to sit down with a CFO or a CEO and say "Let me demonstrate to you that if we improve retention by X percent or if we improve this aspect of the employee experience by Y percent, this is what the business result will look like." It could be done with all sorts of metrics, but what's necessary is to talk in their language.

It's especially important because some leaders still think that employee experience is woo-woo, touchy-feely stuff. They haven't made the connection to business results, so we have to make it for them. There are solid metrics that you can go after and show—on whatever cadence that works for your business—the direct correlation such that if you invest in the employee experience, it will have an impact on your top and bottom line.

What would those measurements be?
A really simple yet effective one is to work to quantify the benefit of a one percent improvement in your turnover. You pull together all of the costs associated with that, and say if we improve retention by one percent, it's either going to yield X amount of savings on an annualized basis; or here's how it will flow through to other business processes to drive X improvement in our revenue cycle. You could flow it all the way down to EBITDA. The specific metrics will depend on the business that you're in, but you have to talk in that language.

Thanks so much for your time and for telling us about the fascinating journey you've been on, Michelle!
Thanks for the opportunity!

Chapter Summary

Michelle's interest in EXD stemmed from her time at Gap, where she saw the potential to apply customer journey mapping techniques to the employee experience.

At Gap, she pioneered a "results only workplace" concept, offering flexible schedules and measuring employees on outcomes rather than physical presence, which was radical for 2010.

Michelle highlights the importance of listening posts: At Petco, she and the Chief Stores Officer conducted partner roundtables, asking simple questions that yielded rich, actionable feedback and built trust.

She established employee advisory groups that co-designed solutions and influenced business strategy, such as the successful advocacy by the women's resource group for infertility benefits.

Michelle emphasizes senior leader visibility and symbolic actions (e.g., "I'm not confused. I work for you." t-shirts) as crucial for building trust and commitment to EXD.

She stresses that CHROs must quantify the business impact of EXD in financial terms (for example, cost savings from retention improvement) to convince skeptical leaders who may otherwise view EXD as "woo-woo."

15 | Making EXD Your Own

Final Wisdom and What Grows over Time

We've come a long way in these chapters! Now we're at the last one, and we have no other concepts for you to learn—only some ideas for you to consider and reflect on.

The previous pages have been a thought journey where we started with what Employee Experience is and is not. We then debunked many misconceptions about it. You've heard not only our stories from the trenches, but we interviewed some amazing people, so you could see how EXD has been implemented in all sorts of situations.

Throughout this handbook, we've given examples of how EXD has worked in many industries: retail, healthcare, hospitality, ecommerce, consultancy, apparel, biotech, and technology, among others. We've also shown how helpful EXD can be not only to the organizations that practice it, but to the careers of the leaders who are the driving force behind the EXD mindset.

Back to Our North Star

We hope we've succeeded in getting across a nuanced message: That Employee Experience Design can be extraordinarily powerful and transformative, but it's not magical—it's fundamental. It's working in alignment with the conditions that create the most growth.

When I (Dean) was at Patagonia, we did many things differently from your typical company, as I already shared with you. One of the biggest differences was Patagonia's focus on saving the Earth. It was not lip service or putting out a few recycling bins. It was a profound belief that "We're in business to save our home planet": Our mission was not about making goods that killed our planet more slowly—we had to figure out how to save it.

As part of that mission, we learned about and supported regenerative agriculture. With traditional agriculture, you open up the soil, put seeds in it, grow the food that removes the nutrients, and then you do it all over again. You might add fertilizer and pesticides and even rotate crops, but this type of agriculture does not preserve the soil—it steadily degrades it.

Regenerative agriculture is different. It's a process of increasing soil organic matter, increasing the biodiversity of the land, doing rotational grazing, and several other practices so you actually can improve the health of the land over time.

> *"As much as I put into my work, I believe that the company gives back equal or greater value to my life."*

When I learned these concepts, it occurred to me: *Wait a minute. Most organizations treat people the way agriculture was traditionally done: They squeeze as much as possible out of them. The annual performance review is basically about what your yield was this season for the organization. Hey, you're getting a paycheck and besides, if you don't like it, well there are plenty of production units who will be glad for the job.*

I began to think about how we could turn Patagonia into a regenerative workplace. That's why we began to ask whether people agreed or disagreed with the statement:

> "As much as I put into my work, I believe that the company gives back equal or greater value to my life."

With time and more data, we discovered that no matter where or what company—this single question was the most powerful indicator of what matters when measuring the impact of employee experience. The initiatives you've already heard about, like travel companions, four-day work weeks, and so on, were part of the effort to care for the precious thing that did all the creation for the company—our employees.

The three of us (Dean, Samantha and Mark) have seen the astonishing power of focusing on employee experience, whether it was at Airbnb (Mark), Patagonia (Dean), and dozens of consulting clients (Samantha), just to name a few places where we've worked and seen it flourish. Once you see it in action, you never want to go back to doing things the old way.

When you think about it, the mindset of EXD is similar to nature's way in three other respects:

- **Caring can be both good for the soil and for the output at the same time.** It's possible to co-create excellent employee experiences and also meet your organizational objectives. Indeed, we argue that it's the best way.
- **Regular effort counts more than all-out pushes.** It's easy for employees to dismiss the latest initiative delivered with fanfare. As you've seen in these pages, the culture changes when employees are involved and over time they see they've been listened to.
- **Growth takes patience.** At first, you put in a lot of effort and don't have much to show for it. With patience, after those new approaches take root, you can step back and see the fruits of your labor.

> *Employee Experience Design requires no leaps of faith or effort—just a steady application of the mindset we've covered and a willingness to figure things out as you go.*

Employee Experience Design requires no leaps of faith or effort—just a steady application of the mindset we've covered and a willingness to figure things out as you go.

Two Mistakes to Avoid

In a sense, the risk is not in the journey as much as it's in not taking those first steps. That risk takes two forms, and here's how to avoid them:

1. **Don't make the mistake of deciding that because we didn't talk about your specific situation, then EXD won't work for you.** Even though we've discussed how Employee Experience Design has worked in a wide variety of organizations, we're certain that we've not described your exact situation. We've found that if people look hard enough for reasons not to do something, they usually find them.

   The trick is to not look for differences, but to look for footholds. Maybe some of our examples just won't work in your organization—fine. Look for inspiration that you *can* borrow, modify, and test in your situation. That's how great progress has always been made—someone sees a thing and thinks, *I wonder how I might make that work here?*

2. **Don't wait until you're SUPER READY before taking action.** It's common to read at the end of a book about how you should "commit" to something. We don't say that, because authentic commitment comes only with time. We're suggesting something that's easier to do: Just start small. Start tiny, even. Plant one single seed. Have one conversation. Create one sticky note about something you read in here that you really want to remember and use. You'll make far more progress that way than if you try to clear the decks and schedule major time for EXD—someday.

You are Not Alone

Maybe you already work for a forward-thinking organization that's more than ready for EXD; in that case, congrats! Then again, maybe you see an uphill challenge ahead of you. In these pages, we've given you advice on how to start small and make progress without putting a target on your back with the next Big Initiative.

If you like what you've read here, the good news is there's a whole group of like-minded people who support each other. We're not talking about some dues-paying association you need to join. It's more of an informal network of people who stay in touch with each other. One way to be part of that network is to visit the EX Manifesto site.[1] We'll be sure to keep you in the loop about any future activities.

The other way is something we mentioned in several places in this handbook: You can contact us directly and ask for those supplemental materials. You might also have a question that we didn't answer. Either way, you can reach us at EXDBook.com and let us know what's on your mind, and we will get back to you.

Thank you for reading this handbook. In the spirit of Employee Experience Design, we hope you have gotten more out of it than the time it took you to read it. We can't wait to hear how you and your employees put your own unique spin on this timely and effective approach to improving your organizational journey.

---

[1] https://www.exmanifesto.com/

Postscript
A Personal Reflection from the Authors

We didn't set out to write a book. None of us needed another project, and the world already had lots of business titles. But what started as a message, a podcast, a coffee, a dog walk, a diagnosis—and a summit in Bhutan—became something we couldn't ignore. It was about building something that would outlast us.

This is how three people with different paths, cultures, and moments of courage came together around a shared conviction: that Employee Experience Design could change lives, companies, and maybe even the way we work, forever.

What brought us together was something much more personal and more powerful. A sense of calling. A shared belief that work could be different. A conviction that the experiences people have at work shouldn't just be slightly better ... they should be transformational. For people and for companies.

It was about making an impact. And over time, it became clear: telling this story, and sharing what we've learned, was one way to do that.

The great convergence began when a tenacious, bold, and visionary New Zealander tuned into a podcast across the planet. The episode featured a guy who was pioneering a new concept at a rapidly growing American company, shifting from HR to EX at Airbnb. That sparked a transformation in her own company based on those same principles.

Eventually, she began bringing together some of the world's most forward thinkers in Austin, Texas to align on a Manifesto for the future of Employee Experience Design.

Her first call was to the podcast guest who had changed the course of her career. He said, "hell yes" and then suggested a second call.

Across the ocean in Santa Barbara, California, the former CHRO of Patagonia was opening his LinkedIn messages, wading through pitches and job inquiries. One message stood out: an enthusiastic note from that same New Zealander about an Employee Experience summit in Austin. What she didn't know was that he was preparing for cancer surgery around the time of the summit.

As luck would have it, she was in New York while he was recovering nearby. They met for lunch at Balthazar and knew instantly that their lives would be on a shared path they couldn't have imagined. Even more surprising? That the Patagonia and Airbnb execs had unknowingly walked their dogs in the same park every day … and lived just a block apart.

This is how the three of us found each other, and how we became stewards of what would become the EX Manifesto and the foundation for a lifelong friendship.

The idea for this handbook emerged slowly, through conversations, shared projects, and one particularly unforgettable journey. By chance, the three of us had all signed up for the same leadership quest in Bhutan. We listened to ancient wisdom keepers, danced by firelight under stars, hiked mountains, and shared stories of our lives. Somewhere between the peaks and the purpose, the idea became clear: we had to write this down.

But only if we did it the right way.

We aligned on a few non-negotiables. What we wrote had to be timeless. It had to be a handbook for action, not just a collection of cool stories. It had to be applicable to both C-suite leaders and frontline managers, and it had to highlight the voices of EX legends we knew.

What you're holding now is the result of staying true to those values. It's our story and our shared framework. And it's our hope that this book inspired you, lasts with you, and gave you practical ways to help your employees, your company, and you … thrive in extraordinary ways.

With gratitude for reading our story and joining the quest,

Dean E. Carter, Samantha Gadd and Mark Levy

Acknowledgments

Dean E. Carter

To the thought leaders and pioneers of employee experience who started as mentors and became dear friends:

- Dr. John Boudreau: Whose book *Beyond HR* set my mindset for my entire career to follow. He's still my go to muse for ideas and thinking out of the box … and I love our monthly catchups, jam sessions, and long dinners in Santa Fe.
- Keith Ferrazzi: Who believed in me and opened so many doors early in my career. He continues to inspire me, challenge me, and whether it's just us, a long dinner with 20 extraordinary people at his home in LA, or a small intimate birthday celebration—I always leave glowing.
- Marcus Buckingham: Whose ground-breaking work on EX and several very engaging discussions set the foundation for a data-based approach to our EX pulse platform at Sears. It's been a delight to partner on CHRO offsites—and exchange laughs and stories over a great margarita.
- David Rock: Who continues to inspire me with new and provocative research on the neuroscience of how your brain works. I look forward to every new release of new insights … and maybe, another chance to suit up and catch a wave or two.

To the real heroes who created extraordinary employee experiences that I had the honor of working and learning from ... the gold standard that other companies aspire to and shaped all of my EX approaches going forward.

- The Sears People Team: Despite incredible headwinds, this team built a first ever, award winning, Large Hourly workforce Daily Employee Pulse Survey. Not just workmates ... are still today my dearest friends; Chris Mason, Ian O'Keefe, and Naveen Seshadri.
- Lisa Lapiska: Who set the bar high for employee experience early in my career. She gave me my first big HR break at Pier One Imports HR, and then my biggest break of all—my first CHRO role at Fossil. She saw in me what no one else could see. She believed in me when no one else would hire me—even in an entry-level HR role. And I am forever grateful for her kindness, grace, and generous spirit that have been a guiding light for not just my career, but for my life.
- Greg Pryor: Who set the standard for employee experience engagement at the C-suite level at Workday ... and for almost every other company. He and his team mastered integrating survey technology that focused EX/Performance outcomes vs. outputs. This led to multiple years of Best Place to Work and other industry awards. Beloved at Workday... and certainly by me and my daughter Grace for his kindness, mentorship, and long-time friendship.
- The Chouinard Family: I need a whole book to explain the unmeasurable impact this family had on my view of Purpose, Values, and REAL employee experiences. I was a student every day ... mostly learning and unlearning years of what I thought was right about not just work—but how I live as a human and steward of people and this wonderful planet.

To my dear family:

- Mark Stori is not just who I chose to marry and spend my life with in 2000. He is my best friend, my supporter, my challenger, and my rock ... at work and life. I am so grateful for the headspace and time he made for me to spend days and nights working on this book with Mark and Sam ... to go to events, conferences, and wisdom quests ... and give some real world practical advice and wise counsel as we finally went to press.

- Grace Stori is our daughter and light of my life, She inspires me, makes me laugh, makes my heart fly, and is my biggest fan and cheerleader. She has started her career on the HR team at Workday and I love when we get to talk shop. Given her career trajectory and impact at work ... I wouldn't be surprised if you saw her name on the author line of a book like this some day.

Samantha Gadd

No one operates on their own. Without my family—Steve and our sons, my true A-team—I would not have had the space to learn, grow, and build.

To Ryder, Harper, and Miller, I hope you one day join organizations that provide enriching employee experiences, shaped by leaders who care as much about people as they do about performance.

To the Humankind team, past and present: Thank you for helping to shape the methodology that became Employee Experience Design. Your thinking, experiments, and commitment to better ways of working have laid the foundations for this book.

To everyone who has taken part in EX Design School: Your courage to apply this approach in your own organizations has been inspiring. You've shown what's possible when people leaders choose to design with, not for, their employees.

To the EX Manifesto contributors (exmanifesto.com): Thank you for helping us define what employee experience is, and for putting a flag in the sand for practitioners and leaders around the world. Your voices have helped build a shared vision for the future of work.

To the incredible leaders who generously shared their stories for this book: Thank you for showing what's possible. Your real-world examples will, we hope, inspire every other people leader to see that EX Design is not only possible, but powerful.

Mark Levy

There are many people I'd like to thank for having influenced me to become who I am.

- My parents, Diane and Jim Levy. Mom is the quintessential Jewish mother, a total giver, cares about everyone and everything, and taught me so much about being positive, being curious, showing genuine care and concern, and being selfless and caring for others. Dad taught me about working hard, having strong and solid values, as well as being humble, reliable, and authentic.
- My family, starting with my wife Lindsay, who is the only reason I could work so hard and be gone so much for work travel. She cheered me on as I changed jobs every time I was not comfortable with the values or leadership at an organization. While I was heads down for many years, 24/7, she was there for the kids and for me, and sacrificed her career for the good of the family. Her patience, calmness, great advice, and support is the foundation of our friends and family. I am so proud and have learned so much from my three kids, Evans, Eliza, and Sam. They all suffered through me trying to bring "HR" ideas to the family. They went to Paris kicking and screaming when we moved there for a job, then didn't want to leave, and were all trying to get back there. They're kicking it as they have entered the workforce.
- My mentors. I have had so many people along the way that taught me what good looks like in so many ways.
    - Lou and Renee at Northstar Camp, where I spent 13 summers in the Northwoods. They taught me about how to help those less fortunate—which I have applied both personally and professionally.
    - Ken Weller and Phil Lee were good guys who taught me how to focus on the business and on employees—not policies and procedures—and transformed the way I looked at HR.
    - Shari Ballard at Best Buy was the irreverent store manager who was paired with me to co-lead HR and we were a force to be reckoned with. She is whip smart and imparted so much practical wisdom on igniting the passion of our people and being positioned to notice.

- Bobbi Silten, who I recruited from Levi's to Gap Inc, has such a big heart, sage advice, and compassionate leadership. She's what inspired me to Be What's Possible.
- Eva Sage Gavin from my Gap Inc days continues to be such an inspiring, take-no-prisoners, HR maverick.
- I learned so much from Paul Pressler, and my absolute favorite boss and now friend, Cynthia Clarke Harriss. The focus on customer service and experience, as well as being respectful and honoring every person in the organization the same, was such a wonderful Disney attribute and helped guide me toward my leadership style.
- The highlight of my career was the Air Fam at Airbnb. I so appreciate that Brian, Joe, and Nate were intentional in shaping the type of company they wanted to build from their first hire on. What a privilege it was to help them create a world where anyone could belong anywhere. Brian, who is an incredible creative and leader, told me my job was to make sure we didn't fuck up the culture, and then I had permission to do things differently. We co-created what is now the basis of this book.
- There are too many people to name at Airbnb who were so instrumental in creating this movement, though I will mention Jenna Cushner, Dave O'Neill, Jill Macri, and Danielle Anagnostaras—leaders of the ground control team who incubated and continue to grow this concept.
- Last but not least, Chip Conley was the guy who told me I was a dark horse for this role yet cheered me on. He was instrumental in hiring me, and has become a great friend and mentor. The partnership we had between hospitality and employee experience, his modern elder wisdom, and his tenacity is like no other.

About the Authors

Dean E. Carter

WorkTech/AI Board Member and Advisor, Independent Board Director, Regenerative Work Pioneer, Community and Impact Leader

Dean is widely known as an innovative and industry-recognized leader of People and Culture for more than 20 years as a 4-time CHRO across Fortune 50, rapid growth, and culture-driven organizations. Dean served in the CHRO role at Guild, Sears Holdings, and Fossil, Inc. At Patagonia, his chief administrator role spanned across People & Culture, Head of Finance & Accounting, and General Counsel. He launched his career through a variety of progressive leadership roles at Procter & Gamble, Pier 1 Imports, and Pearle Vision.

He has served as a public company independent director and chair of both Governance and Comp Committees for Cornerstone OnDemand (NASDAQ: CSOD) and is an independent Director for Griffith Foods, a Chicago-based privately held sustainable food company. He also served on Advisory Boards for numerous HR tech and AI startups.

During his career, Dean's perspectives on innovation in the future of work, purpose-driven companies, and a regenerative approach to employee experiences have been featured in *The Economist, NBC Nightly News, HRBrew, Harvard Business Review, Forbes, CNBC, Fast Company, Inc. Magazine, NPR Morning Edition, NPR Marketplace, and The Wall Street Journal*, as well as a range of books and other national publications. Dean is also a frequent guest lecturer at renowned universities such as the USC Marshall School of

Business, UCLA Anderson School of Business, Columbia Business School, the Stanford School of Business, and The University of Texas at Austin McCombs School of Business.

Dean earned his undergraduate degree from The University of Texas at Austin and currently serves as a Northwestern University Pritzker School of Law Workforce Science Fellow, where he co-founded a world-class organization focused on the elevation of Human Capital Analytics, as well as on the advisory boards for The Allen Institute for Brain Science and the UnivSanFrancisco MBA Program for AI+HR.

With a lifelong commitment to contribute to his home communities and the arts, Dean served as a board member of the world-renowned classical music institute, The Music Academy, based in Montecito, CA.

In 2000, he married his best friend and partner in life, Mark Stori. Their wonderful daughter, Grace, is so ready to take on the world with a big heart and smile.

Samantha Gadd

Founder of Humankind and EX Design School, Employee Experience Design Pioneer

Samantha Gadd is a globally recognized thought leader in Employee Experience Design and an advocate for human-centered workplaces. For more than 20 years, her work has focused on helping organizations achieve performance through people, always with the belief that employees are key stakeholders in the success of any business.

In 2012, Samantha founded Humankind, now New Zealand's leading HR consultancy, which has partnered with more than 1,300 organizations over the past 13 years. In 2020 she created EX Design School, a global certification that equips leaders and practitioners with the skills and tools to design high-performing workplaces people love.

In 2022, Samantha led the EX Manifesto Project (exmanifesto.com), bringing together leaders and practitioners from more than 30 countries to define and advance the field of EX. This manifesto has since become a guiding reference point for organizations and leaders worldwide.

Her work has always been deeply collaborative—shaped with colleagues, clients, and a growing global community of EX designers. Based in

New Zealand, Samantha is also the proud mum of three sons, who keep her grounded and remind her daily of the future we're all designing for.

Mark Levy

EX Advisor and Pioneer of Employee Experience

Mark is a seasoned globally minded Employee Experience Leader who has chosen to work for big-hearted companies and focus on how he and his team can unleash the talents and passions of a company's employees through doing things with—not to—them. Early in his career, he worked with the likes of Best Buy, Levi Strauss & Company, and Gap Inc. partnering with business leaders to support their HR needs including innovative ways to create a learning organization and ensure integration between work and life.

Mark also spent two years living and working in Paris for Thomson/Technicolor.

Mark was the pioneer of this shift from HR to Employee Experience, along with the founders and his team at Airbnb. EXD has since created significant changes in the way organizations globally are looking at expanding the HR function to focus on the entire employee journey and to co-design the experience with the employees. Glassdoor recognized Mark and his team's work by naming them the #1 Place to Work in 2016.

Mark has taken his learnings to advise companies, from start-ups to large global brands, on how to evolve from HR to Employee Experience, how to create an integrated internal and external brand, how to bring the mission and values to life, and how to create a greater connection between the company and their employees, between employees, with the company's customers, as well as the communities in which they operate through social impact.

Mark partnered with Samantha Gadd to help create the EX Manifesto, which is a foundation of this book. More recently, Mark has joined the board of Abroad.io to help others learn more about and integrate wisdom cultures into their personal and professional leadership, as well as supporting Airbnb.org to reunite alumni to their cause.

Mark is happily married to Lindsay, and is the father of three amazing kids he is so proud of, and is inspired every day by their rimposhe 14-year-old chocolate lab, Kona.

Index

A
Airbnb, 11, 18, 22
   Core Values Council, 33
   culture of, 80, 85–86
   Employee Value Proposition, 52–54
   "First Thursdays" program, 93
   Ground Control, 29, 30
annual employee surveys, 17
Apple, 18, 110, 112, 135, 146
   Safari browser, 124
Applicant Tracking System (ATS), 56, 57, 119
Async by Default, 149–151
ATS. *See* Applicant Tracking System (ATS)
attraction, 22

B
BASIC test, 59
Bhusri, Aneel, 180
Bonfilio, Michelle, 189–203
bounce rate, 124
British Design Council, 110
   Double Diamond Model. *See* Double Diamond Model
Bush, Michael
   Great Place to Work For All, A, 179

C
Carter, Dean, 5, 23, 27, 84–85, 169, 206, 212
ChatGPT, 36

Chesky, Brian
   "Don't Fuck Up the Culture", 11
Chipper, 80–81
Chouinard, Yvon, 23, 81
co-creation, 18, 33, 37, 38, 46, 53, 56, 144, 189, 207, 217
collaboration, 15, 19, 37–39, 42, 149, 150, 151, 154
communication, 67–69, 71, 75, 152, 185
   nonverbal, 131
Community Captains, 96
confirmation bias, 60, 119
culture, 28–31, 79–86
customer retention, 147
Cutts, Matt, 97

D
Dauten, Dale
   Max Strategy, The, 94
Davenport, Tom
   Analytics at Work, 169
Define phase of Double Diamond Model, 120–128
   data, 120
   discrepancies, 123–124
   information, 120–121
   insights, 121
   observation, 121–122
   people's involvement, 122–123
   personas, 126

Define phase of Double Diamond (*continued*)
  problem statement, 126–128
  themes and patterns, 124–126
DEI initiatives, 12, 112
Deliver phase of Double Diamond
  Model, 133–135
design, 87–108
  brief, 88–89, 98, 127
  "design for them" approach, 39
  design with, 57–58
  importance of, 87
  PREP Framework. *See* PREP
    Framework
Design phase of Double Diamond
  Model, 128–133
  getting ideas over time, 131–132
  with Minimum Viable Product, 132
  testing, 133
Dewey, John, 126
Discover phase of Double Diamond
  Model, 111–120
  desk research, 114
  interviews, 113
  journey mapping, 114–118
  market and competitor analysis, 118–120
  observation, 113
  user research, 113
  wide *versus* narrow, 120
discovery process, 67–70, 73, 74
Double Diamond Model, 104, 109–136,
  139, 143, 161
  Define phase of, 120–128
  Deliver phase of, 133–135
  Design phase of, 128–133
  Discover phase of, 111–120
Dropbox, 146–148, 151, 153
Dropbox Virtual First, 145, 148, 150, 151,
  153–154, 158
Drucker, Peter, 49
Duffield, Dave, 183
Duhigg, Charles
  Power of Habit, The, 27

E
Einstein, Albert, 8, 11
Ellis, Shannon, 25

emotions, 60
empathy, 32, 60
  mapping, 118
Employee Experience (EX), 36–38. *See also
  individual entries*
  Blueprint, 139–144
  definition of, 10
  distinguished from HR, 43, 65
  key questions, 206–207
  misconceptions about, 38–42
  projects, GPS navigation for,
    162–173
  success measurement, 42–43
Employee Experience Design (EXD).
    See also individual entries
  definition of, 10
  emotional core of, 189–203
  guiding principle, 21–34
  important aspects of, 70, 154
  initiatives, 25–26
  mindsets for, 49–61
  misunderstandings of, 155
  myths of, 155
employees
  definition of, 9
  engagement, 24, 29, 41, 75, 119, 121, 125,
    147, 148, 151, 152, 154, 158, 166, 172,
    175, 191, 196, 214
  interactions with, 67
  retaining, 23–25
  retention, 14, 24, 25, 34, 39, 51, 75, 151,
    152, 154, 183, 191, 192, 194,
    202, 203
Employee Value Proposition (EVP), 42,
  52–55, 60, 148
engagement, 24, 69
  employee, 29, 41, 75, 119, 121, 125, 147,
    148, 151, 152, 154, 158, 166, 172, 175,
    191, 196, 206–207, 214
  surveys, 102, 154, 161, 174, 182,
    206–207
EVP. *See* Employee Value Proposition (EVP)
EX. *See* Employee Experience (EX)
EXD. *See* Employee Experience
  Design (EXD)
EX Manifesto, 209, 212

Index

F

feedback, 11, 13, 37, 44–46, 58, 68, 70–72, 75, 131, 134, 136, 148, 154, 157, 158, 179, 180, 182, 183, 185, 186, 194, 197, 200, 201, 203
- constructive, 100
- direct, 72
- honest, 165, 174
- regular, 100

Feedback Fridays, 179, 182, 183, 185, 186
"5 Whys" technique, 119, 121, 135
flare thinking, 112, 120, 135
focus thinking, 135
Fossil, Inc., 85
Four-day Work Week, 34, 207

G

Gabree, Matt, 37
Gadd, Samantha, 5, 212
Gap Inc. 54
Gap Inc Direct (GID), 192, 193
GE, 146
Generate:Biomedicines, 36
generative biology, 36
GID. *See* Gap Inc Direct (GID)
GPS navigation, for EX projects, 162–173
- baseline and measurement, 164–165
- honest feedback, 165
- information gathering, 164–168
- metrics, 164
- questions, 163, 166, 168–171
- review of questions, 166
- statistical significance, 167–168
- survey, 164, 167, 172

Groundhog Day, 135
Grous, Beth, 35–46
Guild, 24–28, 96, 171, 174

H

Haka House, 63, 64, 104, 163
Hart, Mickey, 55
Help at Home, LLC, 190, 199–200
Hout, Thomas M.
- *Competing Against Time*, 53–54

HR. *See* human resource (HR)

HRPS Advisory Board, 35
human resource (HR), 44–45
- distinguished from Employee Experience, 43, 65

I

iteration, 58–59

J

Jobs, Steve, 10, 18
Jucy Rentals, 64
Juniper Networks, 176–178

K

Kaufer, Steve, 37
Key Performance Indicators (KPIs), 91, 94, 195
Kickstarter campaign, 21
kindness, 59–60
"Know, Think, Suspect" workshops, 65–67, 69, 102–105, 107, 108, 163
KPIs. *See* Key Performance Indicators (KPIs)
Kriens, Scott, 176, 177

L

lagging indicators, 121
leading indicators, 121, 174
LEGO, 110, 135
Levy, Mark, 5, 212
Lloyd, Kirsty, 63–75, 163

M

Massachusetts Institute of Technology, 171
metrics, 161–174
Microsoft, 110, 112, 135
mindsets, 49–61
Minimum Viable Product (MVP), 58, 132, 133, 136, 156
mistakes, avoiding, 208
moments
- importance of, 79–83
- of truth, 83–86

moments that matter, 80–82
mutual value, 56

Index

MVP. *See* Minimum Viable Product (MVP)
mystery shopping, 118

N
Next Gen Advisory Group, 198
non-judgmental approach, 60, 112

O
OKR, 180

P
Partner Resource Groups (PRGs), 198
Patagonia, 14, 18, 23–25, 34, 39, 52–54, 58, 80–82, 84–86, 92, 123, 206, 207, 212
path of least resistance, 50–51
People Analytics function, 155–156
performance improvement, 27–28
performance management, 156, 157, 178
Petco, 191–192, 195–201, 203
physical workspace, 53
positioned to notice, 99–100
PREP Framework, 89–109
 enabling experiences in, 97–100
 performance experiences in, 100–107
 purpose experiments in, 90–94
 relationship experiences in, 94–97
PRGs. *See* Partner Resource Groups (PRGs)
Procter & Gamble, 27, 125, 219
product development, 26, 118
product ideas, 26–27
productivity, 23, 24, 42–44, 58, 89, 98, 148, 152
Pryor, Greg, 175–186
"pulse" approach, 182

Q
quality movement, 12

R
ratings, 66
RCs. *See* recruiting coordinators (RCs)
recruiting coordinators (RCs), 27–28
Red Team, 133

regenerative agriculture, 206
regenerative work, 206
remote work, 12, 148
reporting, 38
retaining employees, 23–25
retention
 customer, 147
 employee, 14, 24, 25, 34, 39, 51, 75, 151, 152, 154, 183, 191, 192, 194, 202, 203
Rhoades, Ann, 183
Rice, Steven, 176, 177
root-cause analysis, 56, 119
Rosenwasser, Melanie, 126, 145–158
Ruddenklau, Tom, 74
Ryan Sanders, 64–65, 71

S
Scott, Kim
 Radical Candor, 96
Sears Holdings, 169–174
small initiation, 56
Society for Human Resources Professionals Association, 35
Sony, 110, 135
Stalk, George
 Competing Against Time, 53–54
Starbucks, 110
success
 conditions for, 177–178
 measurement, 42–43

T
test, 58–59
Toyota, 12
Toyota Motor Company, 12, 119
Traveling Companion Benefit, 25, 34, 53, 207
TripAdvisor, 35–41, 43
tuition reimbursement process, 116–117, 141
Twain, Mark, 9

W
why, finding, 56–57, 98
Workday, 178–180
Wozniak, Steve, 18